Alaska From the Inside Out:

Memories of Suzanne Nuyen Henning

SALLY MAHIEU

PAGE PUBLISHING, INC.
New York, NY

First originally published by Page Publishing, Inc. 2016

ISBN 978-1-68409-025-9 (Paperback)
ISBN 978-1-68409-026-6 (Digital)

Printed in the United States of America

DEDICATION

In memory of Gordon and Jane Nuyen, without whom this story could not have been written.

ACKNOWLEDGEMENTS

I NEED TO THANK ALL MY family and friends who have patiently endured the writing of this book. My husband who has been my constant encourager. My sister who patiently answered all my questions, and most of all my incredibly knowledgeable technology advisor, Nick Folkers. Without him, this manuscript would still be a large pile of papers on my desk.

I F I'M GOING TO TELL you about my life in Alaska, I need to start at the very beginning. The story starts in October of 1966 when I met Jerry Henning for the first time.

We met while we both worked at Gilmore's Department Store in Kalamazoo, Michigan. He worked in package pickup, and I worked in the handkerchief department. The first night I saw him, I thought he was really nice-looking, so of course, as teenage girls did, I watched him closely every time he came to pick up a package from my department. We began to talk to each other, and then one night, he asked me if I had a dime he could borrow so he could call his father and ask for a ride home. Later we always laughed about that—because he never repaid me that dime.

On the very day we met, he had also signed up for a four-year stint in the US Air Force. But before he had to leave for boot camp, he asked me out. We went out to dinner and to see a movie, *Dr. Zhivago*. (I still love that movie.)

The day after our first date, he left for Indianapolis, Indiana, for his induction process into the air force. I went down to the bus station in Kalamazoo to see him off, and that was where I met my future in-laws for the first time.

Over the next four years, Jerry and I corresponded, and then whenever he came home on leave, we dated. In 1969 I even took a flight up to Alaska to visit him while he was stationed at Wildwood Air Force Base in Kenai, Alaska.

There he met me at the airport in Anchorage and we drove down to Kenai and I stayed at a little apartment there. He had several days off, so we did a lot of sightseeing. We visited two beautiful and ornate Russian Orthodox churches, one in Kenai and one in Ninilchik. We also went digging for clams at Clam Gulch, and we did some fishing along the way down to Homer. He even took me to the Salty Dog Saloon, which is a famous bar in Alaska, and we had lots of fun.

We visited Seward and Bird Creek, where Jerry took me to the Bird Cage, another well-known bar in Alaska. On the way back to Kenai, we stopped and checked out Portage Glacier. That was my first time to ever see any of the natural sights of Alaska up close. I remember it was blue ice and very cold.

After Jerry was discharged from the air force in 1970, he rented a homestead down near Ninilchik. He stayed there for the winter, and in the spring, he took a job with the Alaska Highway Department. He got a property homestead on the road to Kennecott at Strelna Creek with a little cabin right on the creek near Chitina. He spent the summer working, and when he came home at Christmastime, he asked me to marry him. Actually, what he said to me was "Gets kind of lonely out there in a cabin all by myself. Sure could use a good woman. Will you come up? Will you marry me?" I didn't have to think twice. I accepted.

Well, that was in 1970, and I had two more years left at Western Michigan University to finish up my teaching degree, so Jerry endured two more lonely years in Alaska. He came home the day before Thanksgiving in 1972, and we decided to get married on January 6, 1973. So I graduated from college, had Christmas, got married, went on a honeymoon, and on January 12, 1973, we landed in Anchorage. This was the start of my life in Alaska.

CHAPTER 1

W E FLEW FROM KALAMAZOO TO Chicago and then on to
Anchorage. When we landed, it was cold, and I do mean
cold! It was colder than I had ever felt in my life. We
checked into the Roosevelt Hotel in Anchorage, and the first thing
we did was bundle ourselves up and trot over to J. C. Penney's to buy
long underwear for me because I didn't own any. I remember, on
the way to the store, I saw a temperature sign on a bank, registering
thirty-two below zero. It was very windy, and I was just freezing.
My first set of long underwear was a two-piece set decorated with
flowers—I didn't even know they came that way—I was just happy
to have them.

Jerry had just accepted a surveying job offer from the Division
of Aviation in Sitka, so we traveled on to Juneau, where we stayed a
couple of nights and then flew over to the island of Sitka—total population around seven thousand. We found a little teeny apartment
just big enough for the two of us on Sawmill Creek Road. It was
kind of dumpy, but the price was right—thirty bucks a month. The
apartment had one big room with a kitchen on one side and a living
room on the other. It also had one bedroom and a bathroom. The
apartment's one redeeming feature was a nice porch.

So we set out to fix it up and make it a home. Jerry built some
shelves and gave the walls a fresh coat of paint. He also built a big
bookcase in our bedroom and a cupboard in our bathroom for storage. I made curtains and washed the windows and all the other sur-
faces. I remember how the red-and-white-checkered curtains with
rickrack on the bottom brightened up the place. I made a matching
tablecloth for the kitchen table, and we bought a bright braided rug
for the floor.

The shower was disgusting even after repeated cleanings with
scouring powder and bleach, so Jerry built a platform in the bathtub

for us to stand on while we took our showers. We finally got it fixed up pretty nice and all clean and shiny. We were happy there, and we called it home for about a year.

I really enjoyed living in Sitka, and I know Jerry did too. About two weeks after we moved into the apartment, Jerry decided we needed a car, so we bought an old clunker. It was a Ford Falcon station wagon, and it was truly a piece of junk. Jerry also owned a Mercedes, which he had stored up in Anchorage, so he flew up there to bring it down. He drove it from Anchorage down to Haines and brought it over on the ferry.

While Jerry was gone, I stayed home by myself, and by that time, I had found a job working as a maid at the Sitka Hotel. What a job! But when you need money, you do whatever you have to do, and you can't be fussy about it. And we needed the money, so I took the job.

Also while Jerry was gone, I'd made a new friend, Fran Conger. She was a square-dance caller, and she invited Jerry and me to be part of her square-dance club. We had a lot of fun with that. I had also started attending the Sitka United Methodist Church, and I'd made some friends there, but otherwise, I really didn't know anybody. So for the week he was gone, I divided my time between work and reading at the wonderful Sitka Library I'd discovered.

Well, Jerry got on the ferry with the car in Haines and went to Juneau. At Juneau, the ferry broke down, and he had to take the car off. Nobody seemed to be able to tell him how long the ferry would be down, so he found somebody who was willing to load the car onto the boat when the repairs were finished, and he flew back to Sitka.

I went out to the airport to wait for Jerry's plane. I was very excited that Jerry was coming home, and as I waited, I passed some time talking to an older man sitting next to me. We talked for the longest time, and I noticed a lot of photographers milling around the airport, but I didn't think too much of it at the time. Then Jerry's scheduled plane landed, but Jerry wasn't on it. The man said to me, "I'm really sorry your husband didn't get off, but he'll be here soon. You just wait."

Sure enough, Jerry came in on the next flight. But the surprising thing was, the next day, my picture was in the newspaper with the man at the airport. His name was Mike Gravel, and he was the senior senator from Alaska. That had never even come up in our conversation, but after that, I always voted for him because he never pushed politics at all and I liked him.

The Mercedes came on the ferry a few days later, and we became a two-car family. Now at that time, there were approximately fourteen miles of paved roads in Sitka, so it was impossible to really drive the Mercedes fast enough to blow the carbon out of it. Also it was a diesel engine, and we had a hard time getting fuel for it. We had to go directly over to the fuel company to get the fuel because there weren't enough diesel engines in town to warrant a separate pump for it.

Jerry's job with the Division of Aviation wasn't scheduled to start until April, so he decided he needed an interim job. So near the end of February, he took a job with a tugboat company that took tugs all around southeast Alaska. He signed on as their cook. I remember going to the store to do his shopping with him. The crew got to have big, thick steaks and the whole nine yards. And me? I got to dine on fine hamburger. So he would go off on the tug for three or four days, and I kept the home fires burning, but I was still working at the hotel. He only had that job for about a month before his surveying job started, and he started working at the airport, so he was home every night. I liked that.

I soon got a new job as a secretary in the Special Services Department at Sheldon Jackson College, a small older college in Sitka, owned and operated by the Presbyterian Church. I liked the job because I got to meet a lot of people. I started meeting students from all over the state, and I was excited to learn about new villages with different-sounding names, like Savoonga, Anatuvik Pass, and many others.

I remember Jerry had bought a big map of Alaska to hang on our wall, and I'd go home and locate those places on the map. It was exciting to me to find all those little spots on the map because now I knew people who actually lived in those spots.

My job really was interesting, and I got to work quite closely with some of the college students. One student, Georgina Elia, worked in my office after school, and she was from Tanana. One day she received a box of dried moose meat from her mother, and I got to sample it. That was the first time I'd ever had moose meat, much less dried moose meat. Little did I know at that time that I would end up living in Tanana for seventeen years myself.

CHAPTER 2

W E LIVED IN SITKA UNTIL April of 1974, when Jerry was transferred to Wrangell. His project in Sitka was finished, but the Department of Aviation was building an airport in Wrangell and needed him there.

We bought ourselves a small camping trailer, which consisted of a little living room, a little kitchen, and a bathroom that you had to walk through to get to the bedroom. The bedroom had a wall-to-wall bed. It was a folding double bed, and by that, I mean you had to fold the bed up so you could get into the closets and the dresser drawers. It was a small camper, but it was all ours.

Jerry left Sitka first because I had to give a month's notice at my job, so he took the trailer over to Wrangell and got it all set up in a brand-new trailer park, and I followed about two weeks later. By that time, we had sold the Mercedes and the Ford Falcon, and we were driving a little red Volkswagen. I drove it right down to the ferry just like I knew what I was doing even though I'd never been on the ferry before.

Jerry had given me explicit instructions to be sure to take myself out to dinner in the dining room so I could see what it was like. The passage took about twelve hours. In those days, the Alaska State Ferry was quite a big deal, and the trip was still quite elegant. Dinner was served at certain hours, and real linen tablecloths and napkins and fine china and crystal were used.

When he had booked my reservation, Jerry had requested a stateroom because I was leaving at 5 p.m., so I was going to be on the boat all night long, and that way, he knew I could get some sleep. So I took my luggage to my stateroom and then enjoyed a leisurely dinner in the dining room, and oh my, what a dinner! The menu included Crab Louis, halibut steak, salmon, and just about anything you can imagine, and it was all served very fancy and elegant.

Now this was my first experience being on a big boat in the ocean, and I was kind of surprised when I reached for my water glass, and it came right up to meet my hand. I started feeling a little woozy then. My dinner, which looked delicious, undulated in front of me. First it dipped down, and then it gradually came back up. Well, I ate what I could, and then I tried walking back to my stateroom, but that took some effort also because when I walked, the deck came up to meet my foot and that also took some getting used to.

Getting into bed on the ferry was another adventure. The way my berth was positioned, instead of rocking me back and forth, like a cradle would move, I was rocked from my head to my feet, and that was just terrible. In a couple hours, I woke up, and I was clear down at the end of the bed. I had been rocked down that far. It was then I decided I was a little seasick, but I got over it and finally made it over to Wrangell. Jerry was waiting for me when I got off the ferry. I was very glad to see him and walk on something that didn't wobble.

We were quite happy living in the cramped little trailer in Wrangell. Jerry went off to work, and I didn't have a job during that time, so I fixed meals, shopped, and spent time visiting our friends Mike and Mary Reynolds and their little girl, Heidi. They lived in the same trailer park we did and also lived in a camper. Mary and I did a lot of things together, and that included a lot of walking around town and beachcombing, one of our favorite pastimes.

When Jerry came home from work, the two of us liked to hop in the car and go off exploring. There were miles and miles and miles of logging roads in Wrangell, and we traveled all of them. We also enjoyed beachcombing together.

There are some petroglyphs in Wrangell carved on rocks along the ocean, not too far from where we lived. The petroglyphs had been there for hundreds, maybe thousands, of years. They were inscribed there by early Tlingit Indians as a record of their history. To reach the petroglyphs was very difficult; it was down a rocky path west of town. But we visited several times and found them quite interesting. Sometimes the tides and waves would break off pieces of the old rocks, and once, we found a fragment of one of the rock pictures on a beach a few miles from Wrangell. We rescued it and gave it to the museum in town.

During our time in Wrangell, we acquired a dog that we named Ruby Begonia. Ruby was a lot of company for me, but she was the only dog I ever had that was mentally slow. Ruby was not very well trained although it was not from lack of trying because Jerry was pretty good with animals and could usually get them to do anything he wanted them to do. Ruby was a lost cause, but we loved her anyway.

We bought a small boat, and we'd go exploring in that on Jerry's days off. Once, we visited a garnet ledge on an island not very far from Wrangell where you could chip off pieces of larger stones. We went over a couple of times to get garnets, and Jerry referred to them as our "family jewels." It was interesting to see the garnets in their natural state.

We often drove out to Anman Creek in the evenings when the salmon were spawning, and we watched bears fish from a platform that had been built especially for that purpose. There were usually a dozen or more bears there, snatching salmon out of the water.

While we lived in Wrangell, my mom and dad visited us. They flew from Seattle to Ketchikan, and then they hopped on a small plane to Wrangell. Now mind you, we lived in this little eight-by-forty-foot trailer, but we always found room for visitors. Mom and Dad slept in our bedroom, and Jerry and I slept on a mattress on the living room floor.

Wrangell was the place where I had my first experience with bear hunting. Jerry's boss owned a musket loader, which had only one shot. He asked Jerry to come along on one of his hunting expeditions as his backup. In case he actually came across a bear and he didn't kill it with the first shot, there would be someone to take another shot and finish the job. Well, he did find a bear, but as it happened, he killed it with the first shot, and the two of them brought it back to Wrangell and skinned it out and cut up the meat. As a joke, they set up the bearskin, complete with the head, in a guard booth outside the project Jerry was working on. It looked very much like a human, and I decided right then and there I probably wouldn't ever be able to eat bear meat.

We lived in Wrangell until the end of August, when Jerry's job was again finished, and then we moved back to Sitka and rented an apartment. We had only been there for a week when some friends of ours, Ann and Ben Forbes, asked if we would housesit for them while they traveled around during that winter. They were already getting anxious to leave, so we quickly changed our plans and moved into their house. As luck would have it, shortly after we had settled in to fulfill our commitment, we found a place of our own that we really wanted to buy. It was a two-bedroom trailer out on Halibut Point Road, located on a piece of property overlooking the Pacific Ocean and many of the beautiful islands that dotted that area.

It was a wonderful place, and we were so happy to find it. The trailer was furnished and was situated on five acres of land, on terrain positioned on several different levels, and our trailer was on the second level. Behind it, way up on a huge bluff, was where most of the land was, and I thought it was one of the most beautiful spots I had ever seen.

But much as we loved it, we couldn't move into it because we had promised the Forbeses we would take care of their house for them for the winter. We bought it anyway and then rented it out until spring. Our tenant was a man Jerry worked with who was originally from the lower Kuskokwim area of Alaska near Bethel. He was looking for a place to live in and asked how much the rent was. He was really surprised when Jerry answered, "Nothing. We'll just be happy to have somebody in there and watching it for us."

The man had only been living in our trailer for a week or two when we received a big box in the mail. The box, from our renter, contained two big handwoven grass baskets for which the Bethel area was known. One was a lady's basket, which had a hole on the top of the lid so yarn could be dispensed from it. The other larger basket had a closed lid, and there were three other small baskets, two hot pads, and a cup and saucer all woven from grass. They were real treasures to me, something I had been looking at and wanted to buy but couldn't afford. I still prize those baskets, and today I am still using the lady's basket to hold my knitting yarn.

Sitka is also a Tlingit area, and we made many good friends among them. The Tlingits are known for their beautiful carving and totem artistry, and I have several unique mementoes from that time in Sitka that were made especially for us by some of those friends.

In the spring, we bought a rowboat, and that provided us many hours of cheap entertainment because we couldn't afford much else. We went fishing after Jerry got home from work, or we would just tootle around, exploring the many small islands, coves, and bays just off the coast of Sitka. In a larger boat, many of those places are inaccessible because there were a lot of rocks, but we could reach them easily. When the weather was nice, we went almost every night. We packed a picnic basket, and away we'd go. We had some great times, fishing or beachcombing to our heart's content. We even found some nice Japanese glass fishing flotation balls on the beach.

Soon we added a small seven-horsepower engine to the rowboat, and we could tootle around faster. I think we caught enough fish to feed us forever while we lived in Sitka. There were all kinds of fish—rockfish, halibut, red snapper. You name it, we would catch it. After we moved to Halibut Point Road, where our house overlooked the ocean, we placed a crab pot (only cheechakos call them crab traps) out front of the house, and fresh crabmeat was always available.

Hiking was another diversion we enjoyed in Sitka, and we did a lot of it. We packed picnics and explored all the walking roads we could find. We explored Harbor Mountain, Green Lake, or Blue Lake. Sometimes we just drove as far as the road led, and then we hiked for a while. That was really a lot of fun, and it was something we enjoyed doing together.

By that time, we had joined the Potlatch Promenaders square-dance group, and we took square dancing lessons every Saturday night. After six weeks, we graduated and became a permanent part of the group. We had fun with that, and we could earn different badges or pins. One of the awards was called the Sons of Beaches badge, and we got it because we square-danced on the beach.

We had a lot of fun in Sitka, and it was kind of like being on an extended vacation. We made a lot of friends both together and separately, and we were able to experience a lot of native culture from true natives.

There is a lot of history associated with the island of Sitka. During WWII, it was a big port for the US military. Mount Edgecumbe, which is part of Sitka, was a large military base and is now connected to the mainland by a bridge. The bridge was brand new when we moved there, but in the old days, before the bridge, people were shuttled back and forth on a little boat.

CHAPTER 3

J ERRY AND I DIDN'T HAVE many relatives, but some of them came to visit us in Sitka. Now when relatives come to visit in Alaska, it's always a treat. First of all, it's a treat because you want to show off where you live and, secondly, because most of them have no idea what it's like to live here so you get to show them the ropes.

We'd been married for about five months when our first company showed up. Mom and Dad arrived on May 18, 1973, accompanied by Kevin and Jane, my niece and nephew. It happened to be Kevin's tenth birthday that day, so I whipped him up his favorite meal—spaghetti and German Chocolate Cake—and we had a celebration so he wouldn't miss being home. It was exciting for me to have family with me, and the occasion made it even more special.

At the time of their visit, we lived in a one-bedroom apartment, so there wasn't much room for company. When we told our landlord my relatives were coming up to visit, he said, "Well, I just happen to have a spare apartment, and they can sleep in there." So I cleaned out that apartment and got it all fixed up, and Mom and Dad and Janie slept there, and Kevin slept in our apartment on the couch.

The first night they were there, Jerry explained to Kevin that all he had to do was say "Gee, 'm 'ungry" and when he said those words, I would hop up and make him a salami sandwich, although Jerry referred to it as "slammi."

So there we were in bed, and Kevin started in. "'M 'ungry. Where's the beef?" That was one of his favorite sayings at the time. And of course, Jerry joined in, so at 11 o'clock at night, I got up and fixed them sandwiches, and they were in hog heaven.

I remember that was a really good visit except for the rain. Now it's a fact that, in southeast Alaska, it rains a lot, and when I say it rains a lot, I mean a lot! It's never a heavy rain; it's more what I refer to as a "spit." It just always seems to drizzle. Mom was determined the kids couldn't go outside if it was raining, and I said, "Mom, they'll never go outside if we wait for it to stop."

When we drove into town the next day, Mom was astounded that kids were out playing. She couldn't believe mothers would let kids do that, but after we had all been cooped up inside for several days, she even allowed Kevin and Janie to go outside and play in the rain.

Jerry and I escorted our guests to all the obvious tourist points around the island. We took them to Starrigavan Park, a campground about seven miles from town, and Kevin fell in love with the place. He could beachcomb to his heart's content. The park is located near the ferry terminal, and we watched the ferries come in and even took them on a tour of one of the boats.

When the ferries would arrive in Sitka, they had to stay for eight hours until the tide turned so water would not be rushing through the narrows. Water went through the narrows so fast the boats couldn't navigate the narrow, rocky passageway, so during that downtime, people were allowed to board a boat and look around. They all decided they might like to take a ferry to some destination so they could see what life on a ship was like.

At Starrigavan, we had seen signs of bears, and we went to great lengths explaining to the kids the danger those signs implied. There was a large bear population on the island, and we wanted to make very sure the kids understood fully what that meant. Although they may look warm and cuddly, bear really aren't looking for friendship.

About the second or third day they were there, Mom went outside to call Janie and Kevin in for supper, and Kevin was gone. I think she would have dialed 911 except Sitka didn't have 911. She was pretty upset, and I think she suspected a bear had eaten him. She couldn't begin to imagine how she would explain that to my sister, Kevin's mother.

Well, Dad and Jerry started off to look for him despite the fact that they didn't know where to start looking. Jerry kept telling Dad, "He'll be all right. He's probably just out exploring." Sure enough, about twenty minutes later, Kevin came in tired, dirty, and hungry.

He'd been exploring down at Thimbleberry Creek and was having a great time, and he'd forgotten when he was supposed to be home.

My family stayed about a week, and we saw a lot of Sitka in that time. We toured the museum at Sheldon Jackson College and the museum at the Sitka National Monument Park, where there were many examples of totem poles carved by the Tlingits.

We also visited many of the historic buildings in town that had been there since the Russians first came. You can even visit the hill where the actual transaction took place when the United States took possession of the Alaska Territory from Russia.

My family was still with us on Memorial Day that year. Now my dad loved a parade, and he was anxious for everyone to be up in time to get into town for the parade. The event had been well advertised in our local four-page newspaper, and he was looking forward to it. So we all got up, got dressed, had a quick breakfast, and hurried downtown to the parade route. We found seats on the stone wall in front of the Pioneers Home.

We sat there in the rain for twenty minutes, waiting for the parade to start, and finally it did. It consisted of a group of veterans carrying an American flag and a wreath, and that was it. It was over almost before it started. Needless to say, Dad was a little disappointed. The "big" parades in Sitka took place on the Fourth of July and again on October 18, which was Alaska Day, the day the United States purchased the territory from Russia.

In September of that same year, Jerry's parents came to visit. His dad came up especially to go hunting, and he and Jerry went off with Ben Forbes, who was a guide. While they were gone, Mom H. and I decided to go over to Juneau and look around. We had a good time visiting the capitol and other interesting places and landmarks. I had never been to Juneau either, so it was kind of exciting to be exploring new territory.

When we were ready to board the small twelve-passenger plane to fly back to Sitka, Mom H. overheard someone say they had too much weight on the plane and they had to take something off. So when we got up to the counter to check in, they asked how much we weighed. Now at that time, I was well over two hundred pounds, and no one would ever admit to weighing over two hundred pounds, so I told the clerk I weighed 180. Mom H., who was as skinny as a rail, announced that she weighed 225. I rolled my eyes and whispered, "You don't weigh that much."

She said with a straight face, "Shhh! Today I do."

Well, we made quite a pair, but we eventually boarded the plane through a very narrow center aisle and my skinny little mother-in-law, carrying a huge purse that must have weighed close to fifty pounds by itself, knocked over every one of the seats. After we had taken our seats, she whispered, "I told them I weighed 225 pounds because they said they were overweight on this plane. I wanted them to know that I weighed a lot, so they wouldn't overpack the plane." I couldn't quit laughing because I had lied by fifty pounds on my weight, but I never told her.

Well, she fretted and fretted about the weight limit. She noticed they were loading newspapers on the plane, and she yelled out, "Don't put those papers on. They might weigh too much!"

We landed in Sitka, and we had to call for a taxi because Jerry and Dad were still out hunting. While we were waiting for the taxi, Mom H. saw the workers unloading the newspapers from the plane and reflected, "Why, if I'd known they loaded them on, I'd have stayed over in Juneau."

After the Hennings left, we didn't have any visitors for a while, and we settled in for our first Christmas by ourselves.

CHAPTER 4

I T WAS REALLY HARD FOR me to be away from my family at Christmastime, but we began to build our own special memories. We made our own Christmas decorations. I bought some felt, and Jerry and I cut out shapes with the cookie cutter and tied them with gold string and hung them on our Christmas tree. I made Christmas stockings out of felt for each of us, and we filled them full of small gifts. There were so many presents because everybody knew this was my first Christmas away from home. Every day boxes and boxes of stuff came from Mom and Dad and my sister, Sally, and my brother, Steve, and their families. Jerry's parents and his sister sent tons of gifts, so we did have a merry Christmas, but it was still pretty hard to be away from family.

Jerry knew that, so he did everything he could to make it a really great Christmas for me. In the fall, when we had been in Juneau to buy a more reliable car, he bought me an early Christmas gift, a beautiful maple rocking chair. I still have it, and it's the one piece of furniture that has been with me every place I've ever lived in the state. It has been my security blanket and still holds a place of honor in my living room today.

In Sitka there were no Christmas tree lots where the Boy Scouts would have already done the chopping for you, so we went out and cut our own. That was kind of a sad thing too because the trees there were not full and lush like they were in Michigan. In fact, they were quite ugly, but we picked one that would pass, and we hauled it home and decorated it with our homemade ornaments and popcorn that we strung ourselves. We bought some strings of sparkly lights, and we made the best of it.

I fixed a huge Christmas feast because Jerry had gone out hunting, successfully, with some of his coworkers, so we had a big haunch of deer for dinner. I baked a pumpkin pie, which was really a treat for Jerry; I don't even like pumpkin pie. I made mashed potatoes and gravy and corn, and I remember I also made my mom's orange Jell-O salad recipe with mandarin oranges and ice cream. So we did celebrate and it was festive and we enjoyed ourselves.

By January, I was working at Sheldon Jackson College as a counselor/secretary in the Special Services Department, and I found that interesting too because I worked, again, with many native students from all over the state plus a lot of students who came up from the Lower 48.

My boss, Tom Pratt, was in a group called the Dirty Dozen. They were a bunch of old-timers from Sitka who were just out to have fun, so on April Fool's Day, they decided they were going to play a big prank.

Now Mount Edgecumbe, the mountain, is actually an inactive volcano—not to be confused with the island the high school was on. Well, the Dirty Dozen collected every old tire they could find and had been hauling them secretly over to the volcano. They had been saving tires for quite a few years, and on April Fool's Day of 1974, they figured they had enough tires. So they set them on fire.

Well, when the sirens went off and people saw the massive smoke plume curling from out of the volcano, they were sure the volcano was going to erupt, and it gave the town quite a scare until the authorities figured out what had happened. The culprits were apprehended, and the Dirty Dozen got into a little bit of trouble over it, but they all declared it was a pretty good April Fool's joke—expensive but funny.

After my job at Sheldon Jackson ended, I took a job at the Sitka police station, and that was a mistake from the word *go*. I worked evenings from four to twelve and only part-time. I lasted two weeks, and I thought that was pretty good.

The first inkling I had that things might not be good happened when I rode my brand-new bicycle to work. I parked it on the back porch entry of the police station and padlocked it. I'd been at work for maybe fifteen minutes when I heard *crunch, scrape, scratch, bang.* A pickup truck had gone by, and its mirror had caught my new bicycle. When I went out to investigate, I found my bike had been stretched out until it was at least fourteen feet long and very low to the ground.

The driver of the pickup was mortified, and it wasn't like he could get away with it since it happened right outside the police station. It turned out he had to buy me a new bicycle, but I never liked it as well as the one it replaced.

My job at the police station was basically to do everything that needed to be done. I answered phones, I was the dispatcher, and I prayed every night that nothing big would happen because I probably would have come unglued. It was also my job to feed the prisoners. Their meals consisted of frozen dinners, and I had to heat them up and serve the prisoners through a little window in the door. It was just a shelf to slide the food tray in and seemed harmless enough, but sometimes a prisoner would try to grab me through the window. It was awful.

The last straw was when they brought a seventeen-year-old boy in for me to book on charges, and he proceeded to call me every name he could think of. It wasn't so much that I hadn't heard all the words he was spewing; it was the fact that no one had ever used them on me. I really thought I was handling it okay until he looked me straight in the eye and said, "I'll kill you when I get out of here." That scared me so bad I couldn't even go back to work.

Sitka was pretty small, and I knew I couldn't hide, so I told them then and there I was through. I took the job because the pay was good, but it wasn't that good.

From the police station, I moved on to a substitute-teaching job at Mount Edgecumbe High School. Mount Edgecumbe is situated on Japonski Island along with Sitka's airport, and by the time we moved there, it was no longer a military base. It was now a boarding high school governed by the Bureau of Indian Affairs for students from all over the state, and when we returned to Sitka from Wrangell, I was fortunate enough to get a job there.

In the early seventies, very few villages in the state were affluent enough to have their own high schools, so parents were forced to send their children to a state boarding school for higher education. There was another boarding high school at Nome, and students who were lucky enough to have relatives to stay with in Fairbanks could attend the public high school in that town.

From the day I started working at Mount Edgecumbe, I absolutely loved teaching. Most of the time, I taught social studies, but sometimes I also taught English. My very first assignment was teaching a ninth grade English class. I remember on the first day I looked up to see a huge male Indian student come into the room. When I say huge, I mean his head brushed the top of the door. And when he came in, I thought, *Holy cow! What is a nice girl like me doing in a place like this? How am I going to make this kid want to learn?*

It turned out that this "kid" was practically the same age I was and he had decided he wanted a high school education so he was coming back to school. He turned out to be one of the nicest students I've ever had, and because he was there by his own choice, he made sure everybody else was listening to me. He would stand and announce to the class, "Be quiet. Mrs. Henning is talking."

Well, that first day, I was calling roll, and since many of the Native American names were unfamiliar to me, I decided I'd just go around the room and let the students tell me what their names were. The first boy I called on mumbled something I couldn't understand, so I asked him to repeat it. He said again, much clearer, "My name is Aggafangel Lestenkof."

I was just sure the kid was pulling my leg. Really! Whoever heard of a name like that? But it was no joke, and he proceeded to tell me I could call him Aggie since everybody else did.

So roll call continued, and soon I came to a young girl who mumbled her name, and I asked her to repeat herself so we could all understand her. She said in a tiny voice, "My name is Aggripina Lestenkof."

It turned out that Aggripina and Aggafangel were twins! I thought their mother must have had something against them to give them names like that. They turned out to be great students. Now and then, I still run into them, and we laugh about our first meeting. I quickly learned that Native American children often have long and proud ancestries and sometimes their names spring from that heritage. Over the years, not many of my students had names as simple as Mary or Mike.

I really enjoyed my time at Mount Edgecumbe, and what I liked most of all was to go back home to my map of Alaska and locate my students' hometowns and villages, many of which I since had the pleasure of visiting.

One time while we lived in Sitka, someone robbed the one and only bank in town. Keep in mind Sitka is on an island and the only way off that island was by ferry or plane. The culprit turned out to be our landlord's son, Hubie. Now Hubie was not the brightest crayon in the box, and he hadn't given much thought to an escape plan, but he rushed into the bank with a ski mask over his face and demanded money from the frightened tellers. They shoved some money at him, and he quickly left the building. But he couldn't get off the island because there weren't any ferries in at that time and no planes either, so Hubie got caught. That was the biggest excitement for a while— until the big fire.

That was the fire that burned the Sitka Cold Storage to the ground. Now a cold storage facility in Sitka is very important because that's where the fishermen take all their fish to be stored until they can be shipped out. The cold storage building was located right down on the beach, and it stood on pilings because when the tide came in, the water came right up to the road and the store hung out over the water.

The fire occurred in the fall just after a big summer catch of all kinds of fish that were waiting to be shipped out. So when the fire heated up, the smell was overwhelming. We could smell burned fish three and a half miles out on Halibut Point Road. The smell, in turn, called every bear in the area to downtown Sitka. All those bears had to do was follow their noses to the big fish fry in Sitka, so there was a huge bear population in town that year. It got pretty scary to see people walking around town with guns. One of our friends lost his dog to a bear, and the dog was tied up on a chain in the yard at the time. The bear lumbered right on in and ate the dog down to the bones, so everyone kept very close track of their dogs that year.

I remember, just after we moved to Sitka, Jerry and I were out for a walk in the woods, and he warned me there was a bear behind every tree. Well, that was enough to scare the pants off me. He had the gun and told me he'd stay behind me and look for bear. It didn't matter! I didn't like the sound of that; it sounded more like I would be the bait. I tried walking behind him, but that didn't work because he walked too fast and I had to run to keep up with him.

After that, I never did enjoy a walk in the woods. To this day, I don't walk in the woods if I can help it, not even here in Fairbanks, where the trees are so skinny and if there was a bear behind them, I could see it.

While we lived in Sitka, we sometimes went to one of the clubs for dinner. The clubs were really lodges or bars, and they usually had live music for dancing. We liked the Kiksadi Club, but the best place to eat was the Channel Club, which had been written up in several magazines. I thought they did have the best food there, and that was where we chose to celebrate our first anniversary.

It seems the Channel Club had been robbed several times, and once, when Jerry went up to pay the bill, he came away laughing. The proprietor had a hatchet next to the cash register, and when Jerry asked him what the hatchet was for, he answered, "The next time somebody tries to rob me, I'm going to cut his hands off." People in Sitka were like that and really did take things into their own hands— the way, I imagine, things were handled in the Wild West.

CHAPTER 5

THE YEAR 1975 WAS THE year my nephew Kevin came to stay with us for the whole summer, and that was fun. I flew out to Michigan for a vacation and Kevin flew back with me and we had the best time. Most of the time, we could find him riding his bicycle all around Sitka, and he got so he knew the town pretty well. He found a good friend that summer in Nicco Holt. Nicco's mom, Susan, and I worked together, and that was how the two of them met.

By that time, we were living in our own trailer out on Halibut Point Road and had made friends with our next-door neighbors, Coke and Gary Oines. Now we weren't aware of the fact that when we bought the place, our trailer was not all on our property. There was an empty lot between the Oineses' house and ours, and our trailer hung over it. We ended up having to have our trailer moved, and in the process, we decided to turn it so that the picture window looked out over the ocean. At the same time, we installed a big picture window in the kitchen, so we had lovely views of the ocean.

The lot between our house and the Oineses' house was owned by a third party, so the four of us decided to see about buying the property and then splitting it equally because their house was dangerously close to the lot line also. We were afraid the owner of the lot would eventually want to build there, and we didn't want that to happen. The man sold it to us willingly and we split it in half and it worked out perfectly.

That summer, Kevin helped Jerry build a retaining wall on our property, but they also found plenty of time for fishing, and the three of us did all sorts of exploring. After Kevin went home, we didn't have any more visitors until the next summer, when Mom and Dad came up again.

This time, they brought Janie with them and stayed for three weeks. It was always fun for us when they visited, and that trip was no exception. Mom would celebrate her birthday during that time, so we made reservations for the five of us to go out with Ann and Ben Forbes on their boat for three nights. We motored all around and in and out of the channels, and when we visited Puffin Island, we stopped at a sandy beach and beachcombed and found a big old rope. So we played jump rope in the sand, and then we had a cook-out there on the beach. That night, we anchored in John the Baptist Bay, and the next morning, we all fished. On Mom's birthday, we celebrated with a special dinner on the boat. We had fresh grilled salmon, baked and scalloped potatoes, asparagus, and I even baked a birthday cake for her. I think she enjoyed every minute of that trip.

The Forbeses' boat was a trimaran, which means it had three separate hulls. There were three staterooms and a big salon. where Mom, Dad, and Janie slept. Jerry and I had one of the staterooms also. There were two heads (bathrooms) and a galley. Ben even let Janie drive the boat, and she really liked that.

That same year, 1976, the whole country was commemorating its bicentennial, and since my family was there over the Fourth of July, they got to see a real parade. Dad declared it much more impressive than the Memorial Day parade of 1974.

Another Fourth of July event in Sitka was the Logging Festival, and we went to that too. Mom and I got into a nail-driving contest. Neither of us won, but it was fun. We entered a rolling pin-throwing contest, and again neither of us won, but we had fun trying. All of us enjoyed the logging competitions because the loggers carved all sorts of clever things with their chain saws and bucksaws, and then they had a contest to see who could climb up a pole in the fastest time. And of course, the log roll contest was fun to watch too. Loggers from all over the area, as well as from the Lower 48, came to compete in the games, so there was always a high-spirited rivalry going on.

When Mom and Dad left on the ferry to go over to Juneau for five days, Janie stayed with us. We had a good time while they were away. We went on lots of picnics and picked a lot of berries. The berry picking in Sitka at that time of year was pretty good, so we picked salmonberries, which grew wild all over our property. In fact, sometimes after dinner, Jerry would say he was going out to graze for dessert, and he'd go out in the yard and eat salmonberries. And it seemed like every time we went out to pick berries for me to make jelly, the salmonberries never made it home because he would eat them all.

We also had lots of blueberries on the property as well as a crop of mushrooms called chicken-of-the-woods. These yummy morsels grow on the sides of trees and are bright orange. They are delicious when they are cut up and fried in butter with some onions.

I remember one time, Jerry and I went to pick salmonberries out at Starrigavan Park, and we put a six-pack of Coke in the stream to keep it cold. I took off my shoes and socks, and we proceeded to pick berries. When we got home, we remembered the things we'd left out there, so we went back to get them. By the time we got back to the park, there wasn't any pop left. The cans were there, but they had been slit open (no can opener needed) by some sharp bear claws. My socks and shoes had obviously been sniffed and pushed around, but they were still there. It was a long time before I wanted to picnic at Starrigavan again after that. But Jerry built us our own picnic table, and we enjoyed many meals on that table while we watched the ocean from our own yard.

The beachcombing right in front of our house wasn't too good. There were a lot of islands out there, and they formed a sort of barrier, so most of the flotsam and jetsam didn't come in that far. The only things we ever found were dead starfish.

Another toy we had when we lived in Sitka was a sailboat. I really hated that thing! I hated it so much I've even forgotten the name of it, but I do remember it was yellow. I also remember that Jerry loved his sailboat almost as much as I hated it. Now the main reason I disliked it was, that sailboat didn't stop when it tipped over to one side because it didn't have any chines, which were the angular intersections of the bottom and sides of a boat. That meant that the sailboat just rolled back and forth in the waves and that always made me seasick. I thought it would help to take Dramamine, so whenever we were going out on the sailboat, I'd take a pill. Well, that was just great! I'd get on the boat, and the Dramamine would put me to sleep, so it was either be sick or sleep through the whole trip. It was awful.

I do remember one time we were on the sailboat and were whipping right along when we spotted a school of killer sharks headed toward us. Jerry was really scared, and that in turn scared me. Well, they got to within yards of us and dove right underneath the sailboat and continued on their way. They could have easily capsized us, and I might not be telling this story now.

It was at that same time when a pod of killer whales chased some sea lions up onto the beach because the whales were hungry, and one of the sea lions was killed. One of the whales was stranded on the beach, and it died there. He had apparently chased a sea lion up so far that he got stuck himself up in the rocks and the sand, and then when the tide turned to go out, he was left high and dry. I think everybody in Sitka went to the beach to look at it, but there was nothing anyone could do to save it. It was far too big to drag back out into the ocean far enough to make a difference.

CHAPTER 6

I T WAS IN SITKA WHERE doctors discovered I had ocular histoplasmosis. I began to notice that objects that should be straight, like windowsills or doorframes, looked to me like they had a curve in them. I called my medical doctor in town and explained it to him. He had no idea what the problem was, but he immediately referred me to an eye doctor.

I saw the optometrist in Sitka, who administered a visual field test and admitted that, although something was indeed wrong, he had no idea what it was. He sent me to an ophthalmologist whose actual practice was in Juneau, but he happened to be in Wrangell at the time for a clinic, so I flew to Wrangell. The ophthalmologist concurred with the other two doctors that something was definitely wrong, but he too had no idea what it was. He ordered an X-ray, and for that, I had to go to Bartlett Hospital in Juneau. So I flew to Juneau and had the X-rays done, but even after he saw the results, he was still at a loss to make a diagnosis, so I returned home to Sitka to my medical doctor, Doctor Spencer.

He scratched his head and said, "Okay! I don't know what is wrong with you, but let's send you to someone who will know."

Dr. Spencer called his friend at the University of Washington and made an appointment for me, and away I went to Seattle. The doctor there examined my eye and told me I had ocular histoplasmosis, and then he asked me where I was from.

I told him, "Sitka."

He said, "No. I mean, where were you born?"

He wasn't surprised when I told him I had been born in Kalamazoo, Michigan. He said, "Well, that explains why you have the disease."

Ocular histoplasmosis was caused by bird droppings. The fungus from the droppings would become airborne and people would unknowingly inhale it into their lungs. From there, it would move to the eye and would literally eat the blood vessels, but people would still be unaware of having the disease because the fungus would eventually die and the blood vessels would begin to grow again.

It would take about twenty years for the blood vessels to grow back, but they wouldn't grow normally. They'd form a knot in the eye, and then the whole knot would explode, causing serious eye problems and possibly complete blindness. The doctor explained that this disease was found primarily in patients east of the Mississippi River and mainly in the Ohio River Valley. The climate there seemed to lend itself to the growth of the fungus. He also said some people who got the disease never developed problems with it. I wasn't that lucky!

Histoplasmosis could be treated with laser surgery, but the damage, once done, could never be repaired. I was scared but relieved to have someone put a name on my condition and to be told I could be helped. I did undergo laser therapy, but I would always have a large blind spot in the middle of my eye. It may have slowed me down, but it hasn't stopped me from doing anything I want to do.

After I abruptly ended my job at the police station, I worked at the Sitka Council on Alcoholism for a short time. One time, an alcohol counselor came up from Seattle to lead a workshop, and we invited her to our home for dinner. It turned out that Jerry had to work, so she and I had dinner, and then I said I would take her out fishing.

We had a little skiff with a ten-horse motor that we kept tied up down at the harbor. So we gathered all the fishing poles and other equipment and set off, and I was planning to show off my boat driving skills a little to impress her. In order to make that small an engine go backward, I had to turn the whole handle around to reverse it. So I did that, but I pushed it the wrong way, and we crashed into another boat.

I think she was ready to get out at that point, but I was laughing and trying to gloss over my mistake, and I said, "That was just an accident. It's okay." Well, we drove out into the sound with no more mishaps and I showed her how to bait her hook with a herring and we began to fish. We had fished for a while, her out one side of the boat and me out the other, when suddenly I felt a hard tug on my line. I thought it must be pretty big because it weighed a ton, but I also thought it was a little strange that there was no jerking on my line. Because the skiff was so little, sometimes when we hooked a bottom fish or a big halibut, the weight of the catch was enough to actually jerk the boat around. But we weren't moving.

Together the two of us worked on getting that fish up for twenty minutes, and when we finally pulled it in, it wasn't a fish at all; it was somebody's water-filled old rubber rain pants. We had a good long laugh about that, and although that was the only thing we caught all night, we still had a good time.

Many evenings, Jerry and I went out fishing, and in spite of the fact I could bait my own hook, Jerry always insisted on putting the herring on my hook for me. One night I kept catching fish after fish, and he had to keep putting his pole down to help me get them in. We were fishing out of the same boat, but on my side, I was catching fish, while on his side, there was nothing. Finally he decided to just give up trying and help me haul mine in.

So we continued to fish, and again something big tugged on my line. This time, I knew it was alive because it started pulling our little skiff around. The boat was going so fast it was leaving a wake, and we didn't even have the engine on. When we finally landed it, it was a huge bottom fish. They were called bottom fish, but they were really rock cod. We didn't have a scale, but Jerry estimated it probably weighed between twenty and twenty-five pounds. At the end of the night, when we finally got home and counted, I had twenty fish, so Jerry strung them up and took a picture of me beside them. Jerry was really good at keeping our table filled with fish or crab or venison, so our grocery bills were pretty cheap, and we ate really well.

In 1977 we decided we wanted to see the rest of Alaska, so I applied with the Bureau of Indian Affairs (BIA) for a teaching job at any location in the state. I got a job right away in a place called Savoonga. So we checked out the map, and I accepted the job. Jerry's job with the Department of Aviation had ended anyway because they had repaired all the runways of all the airports in southeast Alaska.

Before the move, the first thing we needed to do was get rid of a lot of our stuff, so we organized a huge garage sale and even sold our trailer and the land it sat on as well as a lot of odds and ends we didn't want to haul around. Then we planned our move.

At the beginning of July, we would load our car on the ferry and go to Haines and then drive from there to Anchorage. From there, we would do some touring around the state and see some sights before we headed to Savoonga. We would visit Chitina first so Jerry could show me his homestead there, and then we'd just jump in the car and drive where the road took us.

As luck would have it, when we were ready to begin our journey, the ferry companies were on strike, so we had to make alternate plans. We sold our car and flew to Anchorage, rented a car and proceeded to go on an extended camping trip up and down the state.

We did get to Chitina, so I did get to see where Jerry's cabin had been on Strelna Creek. But since he hadn't made any improvements to it in the requisite number of years, the land had reverted to the university, and the cabin had been torn down.

We continued from Chitina on to McCarthy, and what an interesting drive that was. McCarthy was an old mining town, and the road hadn't been improved or even worked on at all. It was pretty bad, but it was a fun trip, and the scenery was beautiful.

Actually, McCarthy is located in the Wrangell-St. Elias National Park, and it is quite a tourist trap. Nowadays, the whole area is well developed, and anything that had been privately owned has become "touristy."

Anyway, we had ourselves a really nice vacation. We had bought a little yellow two-man tent that we camped in as we traveled the state, and we managed to see a big part of it that year. We visited Valdez, and Jerry showed me the road he'd helped to build. We camped in a lot of wonderfully picturesque spots, each one more beautiful than the one before. It was my first time to see Denali Park and Mount McKinley. It was awesome then, and it never fails to fill me with wonder each time I see it again—and I have seen it dozens of times over my years of living here.

We spent our time just traveling and sightseeing, and then we had to go back to Anchorage and reality. From there, we flew off to our next adventure in Savoonga.

PART II

SAVOONGA SAGA

O N August 16, 1977, we boarded a Wein Airline plane in Anchorage and flew to Nome and arrived at eight in the morning. At that time, there were six different time zones within the state of Alaska, so we had already lost some hours by the time we got there.

We were really tired by that time, so we decided to find a room and get some sleep. We found the Polaris Hotel, and being too tired to look any further, we checked in. The word *hotel* is much too fancy a name for this establishment. We had to share a bathroom, and our room, which wasn't much bigger than a closet, was complete with two beds that looked suspiciously like old hospital beds. In fact, they actually had hand cranks on the ends for changing positions. We just crawled in and went to sleep.

Later that evening, after a good nap, we decided to look over the town and get a pizza for supper. We strolled down Front Street in Nome and went into Bullwinkle's Pizza and placed our order. We were eating and talking when an announcement on the radio notified all of America that Elvis Presley was dead. That put a damper on our pizza party, and we walked solemnly back to the Polaris and slept away the rest of the night in our lovely hospital beds.

The next morning, I was to report to the BIA office, which was in the post office building at the other end of Front Street. Now at that time, in Nome, there were only three or four bars, and one of them was called the Board of Trade and referred to locally as the BOT. It was a notorious place to Alaskans, known for hard drinking and frequent bar fights, and I had heard of it before. So I was gawking in the windows, not paying any attention to anything else, when a man suddenly ran out of the bar and vomited right at my feet. I was totally grossed out, but Jerry was laughing like a hyena. He pulled me to one side, and we continued on our way. So that was our inauspicious welcome to the town, and ever since then, I've never really cared much for the city of Nome.

I finished my business at the BIA, and since we had to stay a couple more days in Nome, we were going to look for more comfortable quarters. We had heard there was a youth hostel at the Methodist Church, so we went over to check it out. That was where we met John and Barb Schaefer. John was the minister at the church and offered us free lodging at the hostel. That sounded good to us, especially since the beds were not hospital issue, so we moved our things over there and settled in.

One of the first things Barb told us was "Don't use the bathroom between nine and ten in the mornings." I thought it was kind of a strange request, but I said that was fine. Well, the next morning when I got up, I had completely forgotten Barb's warning, and I trotted down to use the toilet, which was really a honey bucket. The honey buckets were nothing more than pails with a board with a hole cut in it placed over the top.

Well, I was just minding my own business when, all of a sudden, I felt a breeze, and I heard somebody say, "Excuse me." It was the honey bucket guy, who had come to empty the honey buckets, and that was why the bathroom couldn't be used between nine and ten. I was really embarrassed, and later I told Jerry what had happened. He just started to laugh, and then he said, "You don't have to worry about it, honey. Unless you take your pants down out in the street, nobody will recognize you."

That was my first experience in a place without a working sewer system, but it wasn't my last. After that, when somebody advised me not to use a honey bucket at a certain time, I remembered.

Nome was an interesting place, and during our stay there, we explored and even did some berry picking. To begin with, the area was very barren, and they had what the locals called the Nome National Forest. It consisted of one lone tree with a fence around it. Nome residents said it was the only tree within hundreds of miles because the land was all tundra and nothing grew there. A lot of gold mining was still going on in Nome, and there were some old-time buildings left over from the gold rush days in the early 1900s.

In 1977 the mayor of Nome was a man named Rasmussen who was from Vicksburg, Michigan, which was just south of my hometown. I was just beginning to learn what a small world we lived in.

We saw the burled arches of the Iditarod Trail finish line, but since it was August, we didn't get to see any dogsled action. The Iditarod is an annual race run in March and follows a historic 1,150-mile trail from Anchorage to Nome and commemorates the 1925 trek of mushers and sled dogs carrying precious serum when a diphtheria epidemic threatened the town.

Finally, it was time to fly *home* to Savoonga. We had already ordered a year's worth of groceries to be shipped up on the *North Star*, a ship that belonged to the BIA, and we had quite a bit of baggage since we were moving to the bush with no idea of when we might be able to shop normally again. So we boarded this little four-seater plane, and after we were seated and I had time to think, I began to be a little concerned. Flying was not my favorite thing to do anyway, and Savoonga was located on a small island in the middle of the Bering Sea, but I had bought a copy of the *Nome Nugget*, so I reasoned that would keep me busy while we flew over to St. Lawrence Island.

The flight lasted about an hour. The newspaper was all of four pages, and on the front page, it said, "Published daily except Monday, Wednesday, Friday, Saturday, and Sunday." So I opened my newspaper and read it in its entirety at least six times, but it did manage to keep my mind off other things, like the fact that we were flying over water the whole trip.

While I was reading, the pilot suddenly whipped the plane around and did one of those sideways things, and I looked out the window straight down at the water. He had spotted some whales, and as a courtesy, he wanted us to see them too. I could not have cared less! I just wanted to get where I was going, and I wanted to get there in one piece, thank you very much! That was a bad experience.

After what seemed forever, we landed safely in Savoonga, and when we touched down, I said to Jerry, "Honey, I'm never going to be able to leave here. Will you build me one of those skin boats? Because I'm not going to be getting on that plane again." Jerry just laughed at me, and I did go out on a plane again. I never did go out on a skin boat. In retrospect, that might have been even scarier.

CHAPTER 8

MURIEL TUMBLOO, ANOTHER TEACHER AT Savoonga School, was at the airport to meet us when we arrived. That was my first introduction to her, and she turned out to be my best friend ever. She took us to our new home, a very nice house that we immediately fell in love with. There were three bedrooms, but one of them had no windows, so we made it into a storage room with floor-to-ceiling shelves—enough space for a year's supply of groceries.

The house came with a washer and a dryer, but I was puzzled over the three water faucets since I was used to just two. Muriel explained we had hot freshwater, cold freshwater, and cold salt water. I thought it was weird, but I soon learned why it was that way. It seems that in the washer, you can only wash with hot freshwater, so all your clothes had to be able to be washed in hot water. If you've ever washed anything in salt water, you know that it comes out pretty stiff and scratchy and smelly.

In the bathroom at the bathtub, I had a choice of hot freshwater or cold salt water. Needless to say, I didn't take a shower. First of all, you can't use Dial soap because the saltwater turns it to mush, so you must use some sort of liquid detergent, like Joy, in order to work up a lather. Jerry always took his showers that way, but I preferred to fill the bathtub with hot freshwater at noon when I went home for lunch. That way, when I got home from school in the afternoon, the water had cooled down, and I could add a little more hot water and take my bath.

One day, shortly after our arrival, we had some visitors, and although I didn't drink coffee, I did the hospitable thing and brewed a pot of coffee for them. After one sip, I could tell by the looks on their faces that my effort had been far from perfect. Jerry drank from his cup and informed me that I had made the coffee with saltwater by mistake. It was a mistake I never made again, but nevertheless, whenever those same people visited, they always politely refused my offer to make coffee.

Earlier I mentioned that groceries had to be ordered for a year at a time. Now that takes a little getting used to, and some things, I learned, never quite meshed, but it usually worked out okay in the end.

We ordered our supplies out of Seattle, and they were shipped up on the *North Star* once a year. The ship delivered goods and supplies to all the schools and all the teachers employed by the BIA in the northernmost parts of Alaska.

I had never placed an order that big before, and it was quite a task to actually sit down and try to figure out how much food and household supplies you might need in a year's time. But my friend Celia Reid Carlson, who lived in Sitka, had tried to help me figure out the math before we left there. She had devised some sort of system for her own use to determine how much oatmeal or flour or other food a body might use up in a year, so armed with that information, I confidently placed our order.

Well, no one, including Celia, bothered to tell me that when you ordered this way, you should always write at the bottom of the order, "No substitutions." Needless to say, I found out the hard way that the company freely substituted when they could not fill an order for a particular item on any list. And there seemed to be no rhyme or reason to the replacements. For example, I had ordered a case of honey, an ingredient for a bread recipe we liked, but when the order arrived, they had sent, instead of the honey, three cases of mustard. One case even had onion bits in the mustard for variation. After the shock had worn off, Jerry and I laughed about our "lifetime supply" of mustard.

Now when we arrived in Savoonga, Muriel had advised me that anything I ordered and decided later I didn't want could be sold at the native store in town. But now she told me, almost smugly, "You won't be able to sell the mustard because the natives don't like mustard."

Great! So there I was with three cases of mustard, but when we left, the Tumbloos bought the remainder of it from us. I'm sure that somewhere someone is still enjoying that original order of mustard.

Another strange thing included in my order was an entire case of Brillo pads. Now family and friends would tell you that I would cut my scrubby pads into quarters because I never used one on a pot unless it absolutely wouldn't come clean any other way. So those seventy-two boxes of Brillo pads were going to last me quite a long, long time. I did, however, find a good alternative use for them. I used them as packing when I sent Christmas boxes to the Lower 48, so my whole family reaped the benefits of my Brillo pads.

I also received a case of tinfoil, and that was a lot of foil and certainly more than I was going to use, so I sold a lot of that to many different people in town. That turned out to be one of the more easily sold items.

One of the missing items on my original order was a case of laundry detergent, so I had no soap for my laundry, but fortunately, I was able to buy or barter that from other people who had received theirs as ordered.

It was a hard way to learn things, but it was effective. I had also ordered some peppermint candies, and I thought I was ordering the chocolate-covered mints with the soft white center. I knew they were one of Jerry's favorites, and I thought they would be a nice surprise treat at Christmastime. But, oh no! Instead I received a seventy-five-pound bag of red and white hard candies. They lasted a long time.

I also received a seventy-five-pound bag of peanuts in the shell. Jerry liked those too, but what I thought I was getting were several small bags. Nope! I got a large black garbage bag full of peanuts in the shell. What in the world do you do with that many peanuts? I started taking them to school for the students, but I quickly realized the younger kids in my class didn't even know how to eat them, and they were eating the whole thing, shells and all. So I was able to teach them another valuable lesson—how to shell and eat a peanut. Jerry and I ended up using both the candy and the peanuts as Halloween treats for the trick-or-treaters.

It was really hard to learn how to order. For instance, if you ordered Dial soap, the smallest quantity offered was seventy-two bars. That was a heck of a lot of showers and hand washings, but ordering just a few of anything was not allowed.

Needless to say, we got awfully sick of some things, like canned peas and canned beans, and what always happened was that the things we liked best were the first to go. That was bad because then from about Christmas on, we were eating things we could have done quite nicely without. And then, of course, during the year, we would discover things we should have ordered but hadn't thought about. Consequently, we had some interesting meals, and we did a lot of sharing and trading with the other teachers, so it worked out fine.

From that first ordering experience, I learned never to assume anything and to be very explicit when placing a grocery order. We lived in that village for two years, and we had a lot of odds and ends of groceries and supplies left over, but we were able to sell most of them when we moved on.

What an interesting education we received while living in Savoonga. We didn't have an electric or propane stove or even a gas range. We did have an oil-burning stove to cook on. Now I had never cooked on one of those before, and believe me, I'd never choose to do it again. The stove took forever to heat up, but if you kept it heated up, the house got hotter than a pistol, so it wasn't a good idea to let soup simmer all day unless you were prepared to open all the windows.

Baking bread in that stove was a trick too. You had to keep repositioning the bread every ten minutes because the bread nearest to the firepot would burn. This was my first attempt at bread baking, so I baked a lot of bricks before I got it right. We could have built a brick house with all my mistakes, but over the two years we lived there, I did get used to the stove, and soon I was able to bake delicious bread. In the end, I was pretty happy we had that stove.

Ours was the only teacher housing to have an oil burner. The electricity system, being fairly primitive on the island, went out so much that we often didn't have heat, but we could always stay warm because we had the oil burner. Many of the teachers gathered at our house when the electricity failed because we could keep our whole house pretty cozy with just the heat from the stove.

We did order a hot plate, so I was able to cook on that most of the time, and it was much easier and much more efficient. I also had an electric frying pan, and between those two appliances and the stove, I managed some pretty decent meals. And I soon found that, in the wintertime, cooking spaghetti sauce or soups on the stove wasn't so bad after all. Not only could the pot be moved further away from the fire so it would just simmer all day, but the extra warmth in the house was also very welcome.

CHAPTER 9

THE VILLAGE OF SAVOONGA IS on St. Lawrence Island, which is located about thirty miles from Russia in the Bering Strait. The island is shaped like a wet rag that has been squeezed out, and the village of Savoonga is located directly in the middle of the squeeze, hence the name. It's from a Siberian Yupik word meaning just that: a squeezed-out rag.

On a clear day, we could see the mountains of Russia. The residents of the village, who had originally migrated from Russia, were convinced that there were Soviet spies on the island who were anxious to take information of their whereabouts back to the USSR. I remember the first time I was told that I started to laugh because I thought it was a joke. But these people were dead serious. After that, I always pulled the shades after dark because I didn't want anyone spying on me. Once, while we lived there, a Russian plane did land in Savoonga, but it was only because the pilot had become lost in bad weather.

My job was very challenging. I taught first grade, and I had a total of twenty-one students all with Siberian Yupik names, like Uninnaq and Vuvu. Of course, none of my students spoke English, and I did not speak Siberian Yupik, so I taught with two teacher's aides, Apiyeka and Sunqaanga. They helped me with translation, and they were wonderful. The kids were very patient, and together we learned. I learned how to understand their language, and they learned to speak English.

My education began on my very first day. "Kumpa! Kumpa!" were the words I heard as I walked into room number 1 at Savoonga Day School. Twenty-one children were shouting and pointing at something. Then I saw it—a big horsefly buzzing around the room. The kids seemed afraid and were trying to get away from the fly, so

I tried to calm them down and had nearly succeeded when the fly zoomed back at us.

I snatched a workbook from a desk and swatted at the fly. Finally, after several attempts, I smashed him. The kids all gathered around and, in their native tongue, discussed the fly. They were pointing at the head, saying, "Noskok," and I repeated, "Head." That was how my first language lesson began.

No one had bothered to tell me I'd be teaching kids who didn't speak English. I guess it just wasn't important that I should know that. It was important to me, though, so we started from the dead fly, and soon I was teaching them words from pictures. They would give me the word in their language, and I would repeat it for them and then give them the corresponding English word. What fun it was for those twenty-one first graders to be teaching their teacher.

We quickly progressed to a point where we could communicate very well though I still had some trouble. I found that slang terms I had used all my life had to be dropped if I didn't want to go into long explanations. One day, we were washing our hands for lunch, and I told Uninnaq to "step on it." She did just that and began stomping her feet as if to step on a bug. I'm sure she thought I was crazy, but being a first grader means having absolute trust in everything your teacher says.

During the next two years, my students learned a lot, but I learned more—more about feelings and pride. They were proud of themselves, and I was proud of them. I think, to this day, they were proudest of having taught their teacher to speak Siberian Yupik. Sometimes when I remember, I can still hear them giggling when I'd mispronounce a word, but they were glad I could understand them when they tried to tell Nuyaq what was bothering them.

One of the first things my students did was give me the Eskimo name of Nuyaq. In Siberian Yupik, that means "hair," and at that time, I had very long hair. Sometimes I wore my hair up in a ponytail or pigtails, and sometimes I just wore it down, but the kids seemed to be fascinated with the length of it, so they christened me Nuyaq.

Occasionally, in my travels now, I meet a Savoonga student, and they greet me with "Hi, Nuyaq." It makes me feel good that, after all those years, they still remember me.

One interesting character at the school was a cook whose name was Kermit. He was always inventing interesting meals to serve to the kids and keep them happy. Well, the kids' favorite lunch treat was something Kermit called spaghetti and square meat. One day as I was reading the menu to my class, they collectively cheered, "Oh boy, spaghetti and square meat!" Then they patiently detailed Kermit's recipe for this treat as only first graders could. It had one bag of spaghetti, one can of tomato sauce, and a can of Spam chunked up into small squares. It came out pink and looked pretty gross, but the kids absolutely loved it and requested it over and over.

CHAPTER 10

J ERRY AND I SOON LEARNED that you pretty much had to make your own entertainment since movie theaters, bowling alleys, and the like were non-existent in the village. As a result, there were some pretty extreme practical jokes played out, especially among the teachers.

Keith Koontz, one of the teachers, staged one memorable hoax that had people talking for quite some time. Out of some old materials he had around his house, he fashioned a pair of really big feet he could actually wear. He put them on and randomly walked around town, leaving gigantic footprints in the snow and mud. Let me tell you, people were pretty scared, and that included everyone, not just the natives.

So one Sunday morning, I got up as usual and put up the shades, and I saw a really scary sight. Coming toward our house were about fifteen or twenty men dressed in camouflage outfits, and they were armed with guns. I yelled for Jerry to come because I thought we were being attacked. He shot out of bed and ran out the door, pulling on his clothes as he went, to see what was going on.

It turned out that Keith had gone just a trifle overboard with his shenanigan. He had dressed in his new big feet and walked all around the school building and then continued over to our house and circled that too. Because the footprints led to our house, the men thought the monster might have done us great bodily harm, so they were out in force to check on us. They warned me not to walk to school by myself because there was something big and strange walking around on the island.

And that wasn't even the worst part of the story. Keith had really stirred up the natives, who were already terrified, thinking that Russian enforcers were coming to spy on them and capture and return them to Russia. So what had started as an innocent prank to spice up our winter doldrums and add some humor to life in the village had turned sour. And although the teachers were able to laugh at the whole incident once it was revealed, the natives never quite understood the humor at all.

We enjoyed exploring the island with the Tumbloos. They had a couple of three-wheelers and often invited us to go out with them. In fact, the day we arrived in Savoonga, Earl and Muriel invited us over for dinner. While we were eating, Muriel announced that after dinner we'd go for a three-wheeler ride and she'd show me around town. I thought it sounded like fun, and even though I'd never driven one, I figured it couldn't be too hard to learn.

So after the dishes were done and Jerry and Earl had come back from their own ride, Muriel and I set out. I explained that I had never ridden one of those things before, and she told me how it was a really simple thing to do and that she'd have me riding like a pro in no time, and then she proceeded to give me the "short course."

"You use your foot to shift and use your finger to give it gas, and that's about it," she instructed.

Okay, I thought. *No problem. I can do this. Just step on the pedal on the side of the machine and push down for first gear and then second, etc.*

Now all the city's utility pipes were contained in a big box called a utilidor, but they had built ramps, so you could go up over the top of the box. Well, I managed to do that with no problem, and although I was going really, really slow, I was impressed with my quick progress.

At the bottom of the ramp, there was a big mudhole, and I decided to give the three-wheeler a little extra gas to get through it. So I hit the pedal with my foot, and nothing happened. I hit it a little harder but still nothing. From her machine just ahead of me, Muriel turned around and yelled, "No! No! Not with your foot. Press with your thumb as hard as you can."

By this time, of course, I was in third gear, and I pressed my thumb down on the gas lever as hard as I could, and I popped a magnificent wheelie. The machine and I both went straight over backwards, and there I was, flat on my back in the mudhole, holding the machine up over my head and wondering what I had done wrong.

From Muriel's direction, I heard sidesplitting laughter, and since that was about all there was left to do, I began to laugh with her. The more she laughed, the more I laughed, and the more I laughed, the further into the melted tundra I sank. Now the tundra, being millions of years old, stunk, and the more I disturbed it, the more it stunk. Finally, Muriel was able to pull the machine off me. When I got up, I was covered with mud from the back of my head all the way down to my toes, and I was dripping mucky water all over.

There was nothing to do but go home and change clothes, and wouldn't you know, that night every kid in town was playing basketball in front of the school, but the only way home was on the boardwalk past the school. Well, those kids had a really good time with that, and one of them asked, "What happened to you?" The story spread through town like wildfire, and now whenever I run into any of my old students from Savoonga, they also remember me as "the woman on the three-wheeler."

Once, when we were out exploring, we found a huge dead whale on the beach, and it stunk to high heaven. That was my first time to see a whale up close and personal. Then in the spring, when the Eskimos went whale hunting in their skin boats, somebody actually got one, so we went across the island with everyone else to see it.

The whale was at least half the length of a football field, if not longer. It was tied up with ropes. They'd pulled it onto the beach, and the natives were cutting it up right there on the ground. The whole town eventually went over to the beach on their snow machines to collect their share of the meat.

The men began butchering the whale by cutting off big chunks of muktuk, the fat layer. Personally, I thought that part was gross. Then of course, they wanted to give us some, and of course, Jerry took it because it was rude to refuse it and then because he had a cast-iron stomach and could eat anything. But I remember the first time I was offered some muktuk. I did put it in my mouth to be polite, but it was so horrible tasting I spit it into a napkin and then excused myself to go home and use the bathroom. In Savoonga, it was polite to use that excuse because, except for teacher housing, which had real plumbing, each house had only a honey bucket, and you did not use your host's honey bucket. So I ran home as fast as I could to brush my teeth and get that nasty muktuk taste out of my mouth.

Watching the whale being cut up was totally amazing and an education in itself. And the meat was not just for the men who actually brought the whale in, it was always shared with the whole village.

It was while living in Savoonga that we adopted our dog Mitch—or maybe he adopted us. He was a black-and-tan hound and just a pup when we got him, and he turned out to be a great dog. We attached a bell next to the doorknob on the front door and taught him to ring it when he needed to go outside. This was especially helpful in winter when it was very cold. Since his hair was very short, he didn't want to waste a lot of time out there. So he'd just ring the bell and we'd let him out to do his business and then he'd come right back in.

He was a really nice and gentle dog, but for reasons known only to him, he did not like the Presbyterian minister in town, Alice Green. Alice had been assigned to Savoonga in 1946 and was still there in 1977. She was an old maid and just did not like dogs. Mitch picked up on that right away and steered clear of her whenever she visited.

Alice was a really cool lady, and she became a very good friend in spite of Mitch. She used our house for taking a bath because we had running water and she didn't. So every Friday at lunchtime, she'd come to take her weekly bath. We had agreed on that time because I was home for lunch and we could visit as well. One day, she arrived a little late, and I had to go back to school. So she got into the bathtub (this is a true story according to Jerry), and she got a catch in her back and couldn't get out of the tub. She yelled for help, and Jerry, not anxious to see a naked lady, minister or not, quickly ran over to the school to bring the health aide, Annie Aloa, to Alice's rescue. Alice was really a very interesting lady, and we shared many pleasant dinners at her home, listening to her stories.

We spent the following summer in Sitka, and when I went back to Savoonga in the fall to begin my second year of teaching, Jerry, who always opted for an adventure, decided he would ride his motorcycle up to Anchorage before flying back to join me. It happened that I had to attend an in-service in Anchorage before I flew home, so following his journey, Jerry came unannounced to my hotel room and knocked on the door, and I didn't even recognize him, my own husband, whom I had just left a few days before.

He had driven up the Al-Can Highway on his motorcycle in what had turned into a very rainy and muddy end of summer. He was covered from head to foot in caked-on mud and looked like a big black blob.

Well, we got him cleaned up, and then he put the motorcycle in storage in Anchorage for the winter, but his appetite for adventure had only been whetted. So he bought a canoe and he gathered up two weeks' worth of supplies and he and Mitch flew over to McGrath, where man and dog launched the canoe into the Kuskokwim River and started off on another adventure. They floated all the way down to Stony River before they decided it was time to go home for the winter, so they flew back to Savoonga. Jerry thoroughly enjoyed that trip and often talked about it with warm memories.

CHAPTER 11

S AVOONGA BECAME MORE LIKE HOME during our second year there as we learned more about the place. One of the things we discovered was, it had a large walrus population. Now the village was a subsistence community, and walruses, being so abundant, were a prime quarry for the native people. Each year in early May, Savoongans celebrated the walruses with a two-day festival. Not only was it a time to acknowledge the walruses, but it was also a time for the people to rejoice that the horrible winter was over and the snow would melt eventually and summer was coming.

All sorts of contests were held during this time for the villagers to participate in, including a blanket toss and a reenactment of an actual walrus hunt. It was a good time for people to play and have a good time and forget about all their worries and woes. The Siberian Eskimos had a really good sense of humor, so the skits they staged were funny and upbeat. They always dressed for the parts in their native regalia, and it was very interesting and colorful to watch. The event involved the entire village, and they eagerly anticipated it each year. Jerry and I loved that celebration, and through it, we learned a lot about the Eskimo culture.

One day shortly after my second school term started, Jerry came by my classroom and said, "Hey, the Akeyas gave me a walrus liver." I was happy for him, and even though I didn't like liver, I told him I would fix it for him that night.

When I got home, I could not believe my eyes. The walrus liver was huge, and it covered my entire kitchen counter. It wasn't like you could just slice it up and have one meal of it; there were going to be many meals from it. So I cut some up and fixed it for Jerry, and he just loved it. He liked almost everything the villagers shared with us, and even if he didn't think he would like it, he always tried it. Consequently, he got the name Jerry Opah.

An *opah* is a sea anemone found up near the shore in the spring. The natives would pick them out of the water and eat them raw. One day Jerry was walking on the beach near where some ladies were picking opah, and they gave him one, thinking they were going to have a good laugh. But to their surprise and delight, he liked it and asked for another. So they affectionately gave him the name Jerry Opah. I wouldn't have eaten one of those disgusting creatures if they had paid me. First of all, it looked like the outside skin of a chicken leg, all yellow and bumpy, and secondly, they gathered them from the same area where the honey buckets were emptied. Nuff said!

Anyway, the ladies loved him because he would eat just about anything they offered him. Once, some people gave us some seal meat, and I cooked it up. I think I probably could have eaten that seal if I hadn't cooked it, but the oily smell of it was so overpowering and nauseating that I could hardly stand to be in the same room with it, but Jerry ate the dark, rich meat and loved it.

In the spring, the people talked about the ice going out. Now the ice in the Bering Sea is like pan ice, and it moves in one big chunk. Sometimes, even in the middle of winter, if a big wind comes up, the ice moves about in a huge mass, leaving water around the island even in those frigid temperatures.

It so happened one year while we were there, the ice had moved out in the spring, and a polar bear was stranded on St. Lawrence Island. We had been told that polar bears were very mean critters and we should not mess with them, so it was pretty scary to learn that we had one in our midst. One day as I was out emptying the trash, I spied out of the corner of my eye a big white fuzzy form headed straight for me—or the garbage can. I didn't know which, but I didn't wait to find out. I made a beeline for the house fast. After that, it became Jerry's job to empty the trash, or it didn't get done.

Some people in the village wore polar bear fur coats, which are really big and warm. One of the natives wore a parka with the head of a polar bear for the hood. They were really magnificent to see.

Whenever the natives killed an animal, they made sure they used every part of it. I remember one time when I visited the home of one of my students, I saw some strange-looking, unfamiliar stuff hanging on the clothesline, so I asked about it. They explained they were walrus intestines. They dried them, split them open, and made raincoats from them because, once dried, the intestines were waterproof. Also, uncut, some of the material could be blown up for balloons for the kids to play with. They truly used every part of an animal.

Fall was the season for bird hunting, and Savoonga was home to a lot of puffins that nested in a bank near the ocean, which was not too far from our house. In fact, we could actually look out our front window and get a great view of the action. The people of the village gathered the puffin eggs, and sometimes they would shoot the birds, take them home, tie the legs together, then hang them upside down, and wait until the birds turned green. They called them, appropriately, green ducks and did not eat them until they were covered in green slime. Needless to say, I was pretty careful about what I ate while I lived there.

Thanksgiving in Savoonga was cause for a big celebration, and a feast was held at the school for the entire community. Turkey was on the menu, and I could hardly wait because I was really looking forward to a good old-fashioned turkey dinner like I'd always had at home. Well, Jerry had gone out hunting with Earl in the morning and didn't get home until about half past four, so Jerry didn't feel like going to the dinner. But because I had been anticipating it so much, I decided to go alone.

I bundled up, made my way over to the school, and got in line to fill my plate. Everything smelled so good, and I made sure to take samples of all my favorites. Then I chose a table and sat down across from one of my students. Well, the first thing she did was sneeze—all over my long-awaited dinner. I was so annoyed I got up, threw my dinner into the garbage can, and went back home. And that was the year I had no Thanksgiving dinner at all!

CHAPTER 12

WHEN WE FIRST ARRIVED IN Savoonga, there were no standard phones in the entire village. There was only a radiophone system, and that was located in the school. Shortly after we got to town, the village installed another radiophone in the community hall, and it was right out in the open. By that, I mean someone had positioned some plywood around the actual phone to give people using it some sense of privacy, but you could see their heads over the top of the enclosure and their legs at the bottom and hear every word that was spoken, so personal conversations were not possible at all.

Earl and Muriel gave us one of their intercoms so we could talk between our homes privately, and we were also connected by intercom to the house of David and Carol Ann Combs, and that worked well. But if anyone from outside of Savoonga wanted to contact us, they had to call the community phone number, and the lady on duty came over to our house to relay the message and the number to call back. Then we had to go to the city building and stand in line until it was our turn to use the phone and make our call.

Now a radiophone is similar to a ship-to-shore phone with a lag time, and only one person can speak at a time. When you finished talking, you had to say, "Over." So the other person would then know it was their turn to talk, and they also had to say, "Over." So it was kind of an awkward way to carry on a conversation, but we managed.

One day shortly after Mitch came to live with us, there was a new lady on duty at the phone office, and a call came in from my mom in Michigan. She gave the lady the pertinent information so I could be summoned and return her call. When the woman discovered the call was for me, she told Mom, "I not go to her house. She have big dog." So I never got the message until I had to use the phone myself and went over to the community building. It was certainly not a very efficient system, but it worked most of the time.

Actually, all the native people were afraid of Mitch because he was so big, but the truth is, he was a marshmallow and loved almost everybody. So whenever any of the natives came to our home, we always put Mitch in the back bedroom until they left so they would feel comfortable.

It was while I was living in that village that I developed an allergy to penicillin. I had picked up a really bad cold and the health aide gave me a Bicillin shot, and I broke out in hives. It was horrible. I itched all over, and it just kept getting worse and worse and worse until finally I couldn't even walk because my feet were so swollen. I couldn't get my rings off either. Both the health aides came and stayed overnight with me at my house. They wanted to send me to the hospital in Nome, but the weather was so bad the plane couldn't get in, so they sat with me all night to make sure I didn't die of anaphylactic shock.

Up until that time, I had always referred to the health aides as witch doctors, but after they stayed with me through the night and were so good to me, I never called them that again. They were very caring professionals. They were in constant radio contact with the Nome hospital about my condition, and with their help, I pulled through.

I guess the worst part about the whole incident was that, about four or five days before this all happened, Jerry and I had decided we were going to go on a fast. So when I broke out in hives, he thought it was because I hadn't had anything to eat, so he cooked me up a big steak, and it really tasted good. Then I developed diarrhea, and I couldn't walk to the bathroom because my feet were so swollen, so I had even more problems.

Tuberculosis was still a threat in the smaller villages of the state because of poor sanitation conditions, and during our stay in Savoonga, Jerry contracted the disease. Although he didn't require hospitalization, the condition was treated with radioactive iodine and other medications for a year and he was pronounced cured, but he always made it a point to get an annual TB test.

The village respected Jerry and his sense of fair play, and in due time, he was appointed as the police officer in Savoonga. In that capacity, one of his duties was to enforce the curfew for the village children. Since there were no modern police cruisers, he accomplished that task by walking around the town, ringing a cowbell. It was an interesting place with a slower pace, and it was like a step back in time in some ways.

One winter, our little island was hit by a horrendous snowstorm. I mean, you haven't seen snow until you've been there. The wind howled, and when the wind blew, it took the air out of the snow and made it like concrete. One morning when I got up, something seemed different. It was dark and really, really quiet in the house. I got dressed and ate my breakfast and got ready to go to school, but when I opened the front door of our house, which opened in, all I saw was a wall of white. We were literally snowed in, and our house, which was elevated six feet in the air on pilings, was totally buried.

I woke Jerry up, and he dug me a little hole. I tunneled out and started off for school. I couldn't even see the building, and it was located only fifty yards from our house. It was still snowing and a total whiteout. Finally, I couldn't fight it anymore because it was still blowing so hard, so I dropped to my hands and knees and began to crawl my way along by inches, just praying all the time that I was going in the right direction.

Now I was getting scared, and I was lost and getting colder by the minute, but I kept crawling and finally bumped into the school. I didn't know it at the time, but I'd found the opposite side of the building from where I had been heading. I don't know how I ended up where I did, but I began to crawl again, following along the wall of the school and, at last, came to the steps. I dragged myself up to the door and managed to pull it open, and just inside, I collapsed on the tile floor in an exhausted heap.

I was just lying there, tears trickling down my cheeks, reliving what I had just been through and thinking how lucky I was to have made it that far alive when the principal stepped out of his office and said, "Oh, we're not going to have school today, so you can go home."

I couldn't believe it! I said, "I don't think so. I'm here now, and when I can see my house, I'll go home, but not before then." That was one time I was truly scared, and I don't ever want to do it again.

The wind blew ferociously on the island. In fact, I was told the average wind velocity, year round, was forty knots. So it was windy all the time, and once it started to snow, all you could see was white. We never saw houses painted blue or red or any other color. There was just weather-beaten siding in grayish white, so the houses just blended in with the snow, and there was no color at all.

There were no trees because nothing grew taller than about two or three inches, and that was the summer's crop of weeds. It was a barren land, and in the winter, it was just plain white and barren. So when people talk about whiteouts, I know what that means. There is no means of knowing where you are and no idea of depth perception; it's just white, and it's kind of scary sometimes.

Sometimes the wind would blow so hard in Savoonga that if you stood on the ice-covered boardwalk, you would actually be pushed along without even moving your feet.

So we had the snow and we had the wind and thrown into the mix was the cold. It got cold in Savoonga. It was not the bone-chilling cold of interior Alaska but cold enough, and parts of our house were not insulated as well as they could have been. For example, we discovered one particularly frosty morning that the wall the medicine chest hung on was not insulated at all. I grabbed for the toothpaste one morning and found toothpaste all over everything. It had exploded because it got so cold. It was a mess to clean up and a mistake we didn't make again.

Another way we could tell what the weather was going to be like before we even peeked out the window was by looking into the toilet bowl to see if there were whitecaps. Whitecaps in the bowl meant the weather was really bad outside. The toilets there flushed directly into the ocean, and one morning during a really cold snap, I even found a fish swimming in our toilet, where he had apparently escaped to get warm.

Everywhere we walked, we walked on boardwalks because the tundra made walking on the ground impossible. In the summertime, the top part of the tundra would melt and turn to mush, so there was an entire walkway system of boardwalks through the town. We jokingly referred to the main boardwalk as Interstate 5.

Daily there were lessons pointing out that life here was totally different than any place I'd ever lived before. One day we were walking to the Tumbloos' home when a little boy of about two came by, dragging a puppy on a string. The puppy had apparently been a gift to the boy, but he had "killed it with love" and was now dragging around a dead dog. That was just the way life was in Savoonga, and I had to learn to look the other way because their idea of taking care of pets was totally different than mine and it wasn't up to me to tell them they were wrong. It was their village, not mine.

One time, an old man named Gologergen froze to death on his snow machine while traveling home from Gambell, the other village on the island. Searchers found his body and brought it home to his wife, Ora. They placed him inside his house, and I remember going over to pay condolences. The women of the village were thawing him out. They put their hands on him to warm him, so they could get him straightened out enough to lay him into a casket.

A few days later, we went to his funeral at the Presbyterian Church, and as we walked past the house, some of his friends were passing his casket out the window of the home. It seems they had built the casket inside, and it was too big to go through the door, so they had to break the window out to get him out of the house.

The casket itself was interesting too. We spend thousands of dollars on beautifully lined, mahogany-carved vaults, but his was just a piece of boot-marked plywood, and that was how he was buried. That was when I found out he *wasn't* buried.

Gologergen's service was held, and then they took him to the graveyard. But it wasn't possible to dig holes in the ground on the island because of the permafrost, so the caskets were simply placed on the ground. Then the foxes would come and get into the caskets and eat the bodies. That was what prompted me to tell Jerry, "If I die here, don't you dare leave me here." I just didn't want to think about being eaten by Arctic foxes. That also made me realize why the graveyard was so far from the town. Again, this was a totally different lifestyle than anything I could ever have imagined.

Once, we were out walking along the Bering Sea, and we saw the northern lights like I'd never seen them before in my life and probably never would again. They lit up the sky like a great adobe city, the way I pictured in Bible times how Jerusalem must have looked. It was all illuminated in greens and yellows and reds. Many times I've seen the lights since I've lived in Alaska, but they were always green. I had never seen the reds and yellows mixed in like that. This city appeared to be hovering over the water of the Bering Sea, and it was the most incredible display of aurora borealis I'd ever seen.

That was also the first night I ever got frostbite. We stayed out so long my cheeks got frostbitten right where my glasses came down on my cheek, and let me tell you that hurt. Even to this day, if I get outside in the cold, it still burns although the brown discoloration has since disappeared.

CHAPTER 13

IN WINTER, OUR MODE OF transportation was a snow-go, and we sometimes went out riding with David and Carol Ann. Often we went up to explore what the natives called the mountains; however, the mountains turned out to be more like small hills.

Most native people didn't go up into the hills because they thought that was where the Russian spies hid out. Our favorite time to go up was on a still evening when the moon was full. It was just so peaceful and beautiful. But I remember one night when David and Carol Ann broke a ski off their snow machine, so Jerry and I went back to the village to get help or possibly a replacement ski. As we left, our last view of our friends was of the two of them holding onto each other, trudging across the stark white tundra. It looked like a scene straight out of *Dr. Zhivago*, the one where the refugees were plodding over the snowy white ground. That was all we could see—just David's and Carol Ann's silhouettes against a field of white in the moonlight.

I remember asking Jerry how we would ever find them again. There were no landmarks and no way to mark anything by a certain path or tree, just nothingness. There was something the villagers called the Tundra Highway, and that was marked with whale rib bones at specified intervals. The bones stick up out of the snow high enough so you could see them. Of course, if one of those rib bones were knocked down, you could get lost and travel in circles for a long time. Sometimes you didn't even leave a print in the snow, so there was no evidence anyone had even been there.

Later I found out that David had left Carol Ann out there all by herself while he started back on the disabled machine. I couldn't believe it. There were lots of dangers out there, not the least of which were polar bears. And there she was all by herself with no landmarks in sight, in the middle of a barren wintry landscape in the middle of the night. I still can't imagine how they found her, but they did. The snow machine was repaired, and the next time we got the chance, we were right back out there, exploring again. That was about the only entertainment we had in the winter.

One winter while we were living there, some people went out on the ice on a hunting expedition, and the ice they were on broke away and floated out from the mainland. They were stranded and couldn't get back until a Coast Guard cutter came to rescue them.

I remember one Christmas when we hadn't had any planes in for three or four weeks because of the bad weather. I will never forget the day the plane finally arrived—it was January 6, 1978. I was looking out the window after supper. It was dark out, and all of a sudden, I spotted the lights of a plane. I just started yelling, "Jerry, Jerry, a plane is coming!" The entire village was as excited as kids on Christmas morning because, in fact, there had been no Christmas morning to speak of since the planes had not delivered mail and packages for so long. We could see it was a big plane because the small planes had no lights. It circled around several times, and everybody in town hopped on their snow-gos and rushed out to the airport to shine their lights on the runway to guide the plane in safely.

It was about eight o'clock at night when the plane finally landed, but everybody in town pitched in to help carry the mail to the post office or groceries to the store. Then at ten o'clock at night, Earl Tumbloo, who was the postmaster, opened the post office so everyone could pick up their mail and packages and start celebrating the belated Christmas the weather had cheated them out of. Jerry and I had to make two trips with all our packages because none of our Christmas presents had arrived before Christmas. It took us practically all night to open our gifts.

That was the night we got our first television set. We hadn't owned one in Sitka because there was only one channel, which was brought to the villages by the state, so the state controlled the programs that were offered on that one channel. Their offering was a conglomeration of all the networks, including ABC, CBS, and NBC. The viewing public watched whatever the state chose and when they chose to offer it. So this year, we had ordered ourselves a television set for our Christmas present to us. We were like little kids in a candy store, and it wasn't long before I was hooked on watching *Dallas* every Friday night.

Anyway, the night the plane came in was really exciting. That was the only thing people talked about for days afterward, what they'd received in the mail that night. It was truly fun for the whole village.

CHAPTER 14

URING MY STAY IN SAVOONGA, I learned a lot about life in a culture different from mine in almost every way. I had learned from my students, my aides, and the entire village, but I felt I was ready to get on with the next part of my life. So when the opportunity came to move, I took it.

Although I had told Jerry when we arrived that the only way I would leave Savoonga was on a skin boat, that was never an option. At the time we lived there, St. Lawrence Island was served by several flying services, and one of those was Ramon's Flying Service. We had mostly used Munz Flying Service, but for some reason, when we moved from Savoonga to Kaltag, we chose Ramon's. We had accumulated a lot of stuff to move, including all our personal items as well as the dog and his kennel.

Jerry flew in early to Anchorage so it was Mitch and I who were traveling along with our neighbors David and Carol Ann and their dog. They were also moving on to jobs in another part of the state.

Now Ramon happened to be coming over to the island the next Saturday with a load of fuel, and for a price, he would take us back. I must admit I had never heard of Ramon's until that time, but David set up the arrangements, and the plane was scheduled to be at the airstrip for us promptly at nine o'clock Saturday morning.

I had been given some tranquilizers for Mitch so he wouldn't be so hyper on the plane ride, and I can tell you this right now—I wish I hadn't wasted them on the dog. The first tiny tremor of doubt hit me when Ramon's plane was circling to land in Savoonga. I looked up to see the plane was a combination of colors, Pepto-Bismol pink and bright blue. It looked as if they might have taken advantage of a wholesale going-out-of-business paint sale. But there was certain to be no mistake in the identification of this airline.

Well, the plane landed, and the Combs and I were taken out to the airport, dogs and all, by the school maintenance man. It was then I noticed the plane was a taildragger, which meant it didn't sit flat to the ground but rather on an angle because it rested on a third wheel located on its tail.

Taildraggers were difficult to get into because of the steep angle, and it was more difficult for me being overweight to begin with. So here came a troop of small-built Eskimo men to assist this big fat lady into the plane. It wasn't an easy task, but finally, after much struggling and pushing, I made it aboard. After we were all in, Ramon threw the rest of our things in behind us. And when I say *threw*, that was exactly what he did. There was no rhyme or reason in the loading of the baggage, and when it was all in, he tossed the dog kennels in on top of everything else.

When I got inside, the first thing I noticed was there were no seats—just a couple of kitchen chairs, the kind that were chrome and padded plastic with high backs. At some point, perhaps when they were new, they might have been stylishly stunning in lime green with a paisley print pattern, but they didn't give a nervous air traveler a lot of confidence. One chair was on one side of the plane and the other on the opposite side, and directly in front of the chairs was the door opening into the cockpit.

Well, David climbed into the cockpit with Ramon, while Carol Ann, the two dogs, all the luggage, and I were in the back cabin. Carol Ann took one chair and I settled myself into the other one and we began to prepare for take-off, which was a joke since there were no niceties, such as seatbelts. So we took some deep breaths and tried to remain calm, and Ramon chose that moment to stick his head around the door from the cockpit. He looked at Carol Ann and said, "Your chair is okay. It's bolted down." Then he looked at me and said, "Yours isn't, so it tends to tip over on take-off."

That was the last straw! I immediately burst into tears because I was sure this was the plane from *hell*, and it was definitely going to be the end of the world for me. I turned my head away, and that was when I noticed I could see daylight through the side of the plane, which prompted me to ask silently, "Lord, why am I here?" That was also when I began to think that maybe I should have taken a tranquilizer pill so I could have just slept peacefully through the whole trip.

As the plane took off, I glanced over at Carol Ann and saw that she was crying too, and in my mind, that just positively reaffirmed my feeling that we were never going to reach our destination safely. The situation worsened: luggage and unsecured items of baggage were flopping all over the plane, and very cold air was coming in through the cracks of the cabin. I dug in my coat pocket and found a pair of gloves and offered one to Carol Ann so we could both wear one glove and stick our bare hands in our pockets. Thank heaven the dog was passed out against my legs because at least that was keeping my feet warm.

We finally landed in Nome right on time, and David and Carol Ann, who had previously scheduled dental appointments to coincide with our arrival time, asked me to sit with the two dogs and all the baggage. They assured me they would return as soon as they could. What could I say? We were traveling together.

Now the airport in Nome was not a real busy place, and right at that moment, it was totally deserted. There wasn't even an agent behind the desk, so I took a seat, settled the dogs, and began my wait.

Besides all the upheaval of moving and the scary trip from Savoonga, I was fighting a really bad head cold, and flying had not been the best thing to do for it. My ears were popping, so I couldn't hear very well. I was sitting there, reading and minding my own business, when I looked up to see an unkempt, obviously inebriated man approaching me.

Sure enough, he sat right down beside me and, in very slurred speech, said, "Ahhh . . . I find you really beautiful."

Since my hearing was slightly impaired from the plane's cabin air pressure and my cold, I yelled, "What?"

He looked at me with red glazed eyes and said again, "You know, I find you very attractive."

By that time, I had had it. I was so mad I jumped up from my chair and shouted into his face, "You get out of here right now, or I'm going to sic these two dogs on you!"

He lurched unsteadily to his feet and hotfooted it toward the doors, and thankfully, that was the last I saw of him. It wasn't long after that David and Carol Ann came back. They still remind me of that trip from time to time. In retrospect, I can see the humor of the whole situation, but at the time, I didn't find it funny at all.

Shortly after they returned to the airport, our flight to Anchorage was ready for us to board. I'm happy to say it was uneventful. When we landed, Jerry was there to meet us with a big bag of McDonald's hamburgers, and we all feasted on them. You never know how much you're going to miss something until you don't have it, and McDonald's was one of the things I missed most in Savoonga. Now I was feeling a lot better, and I was ready to begin the next chapter of my teaching career.

PART III
ANCHORAGE-KALTAG SAGA

B Y THE TIME I ARRIVED in Anchorage, Jerry had already rented an apartment for us in the Muldoon area. It was a small one-bedroom apartment with a kitchen/living room combination, and it had a big bathroom, which took up about half of the apartment. But we were pretty happy there, and it was only for the summer and not forever, so it was all right.

I had decided that since we were going to have to live in Anchorage that summer so Jerry could be close to a doctor because of his thyroid problems, I would take the opportunity to go back to school to work toward my master's degree. So I enrolled at UA Anchorage and started classes again, which I really enjoyed, and Jerry worked on a tugboat in the harbor. The tug escorted the big container ships into the harbor to dock, and he was in hog heaven doing that because he had always liked working on the water. I had never lived in a place as big as Anchorage, and although I'd never want to live there again, I was able to complete my education goals.

Sometime in June, Mom and Dad drove up from Michigan in their conversion van, and they brought Janie and Kevin with them but left Kevin in Sitka on the way up so he could visit his friend Nicco. When they got into Palmer, they called me from the grocery store, and I hopped in the car and went out to the first overpass on the highway to meet them. I was so excited, and here they came down the street. When they saw me, they flashed their lights and blew the horn. What a celebration! We all managed to smoosh into our little apartment. We had wall-to-wall people sleeping in there, but it was worth it just to have family visiting again.

Later during their stay, Mom and Dad drove up to Fairbanks in their van, and Janie stayed with Jerry and me. That was the time Mom fell down and had to go to the hospital in Fairbanks and came home on crutches. Nothing was broken, but she sprained her ankle so that slowed her down a little. After they came back to our house, Kevin flew into Anchorage from Sitka and we picked him up at the airport and they all stayed for a couple more weeks.

When Mom, Dad, and Kevin left for home, they decided to ship their vehicle on the SeaLand container ship, fly to Seattle, and pick it up there. Janie stayed with Jerry and me for the rest of the summer, and oh, we had a ball. What a fun kid. She was eleven then, and everything was so exciting to her. Every time Jerry had a few days off in a row, we'd hop in the car and go camping. There weren't many places around Anchorage we didn't explore that year. We went up as far as Denali and then over to Glenallen and Tok. We went camping every chance we got, and we all enjoyed it.

We were camping at the north fork of the Chulitina River, and Janie and I were in the river, walking, when she lost one of her sandals. She couldn't get it, and it was being carried swiftly downriver. She was so upset, and all I could do was laugh. We did eventually rescue the thong although, to this day, Janie claims I tried to drown her in the process.

The next night, we camped near Denali in a little turnoff. We had a Volkswagen van that we had fixed up for camping, so there was a bed in it. Janie and I shared that, while Jerry slept on the floor.

In the morning, I woke to shouts of "Suey! Suey! Wake up." When I did, I saw a moose looking right in the window at us. She was both excited and amazed to see such a big creature checking us out. We had a lot of fun camping and exploring Alaska that summer.

I also did a lot of sewing for Janie in my spare time, and she even got to go to college. She accompanied me to my classes, and all the students loved her. She became our guinea pig for all the different test projects we were required to do for our grades.

I remember once, while Jerry was working, I promised to take Janie to 31 Flavors for ice cream, and I let her pick out whatever she wanted. She ordered something called the Mount Olympus, which had multiple scoops of ice cream and thick rivers of chocolate. And although she looked like she had more chocolate and ice cream on herself than anywhere else, she managed to eat the whole thing, but I recall she felt a little under the weather for the rest of the night.

My favorite place to eat in Anchorage was Skipper's, a fast-food fish place. I love clams, and they had the best at the time. Lots of times when Jerry was working, Janie and I would go out and have Skipper's and then finish at 31 Flavors, but she never attempted the Mount Olympus again, settling instead for an ice cream cone.

Early in September, we moved to another apartment in Anchorage in a quieter neighborhood on the corner of Strawberry and C. It was located in a parklike area, and we liked it there. Our next-door neighbors were an interesting couple. He was sixty-seven and she was nineteen and he informed us he had gone to the Philippines to buy her. Later she told me in private the only reason she married him was to get out of the Philippines but that when you committed to that type of marriage, you would have to do so for a certain number of years. She confessed that as soon as that time was up, she was leaving, but she wanted to have a baby so she would be assured of staying in the United States because the child would be a US citizen.

It was my Filipina neighbor who taught me how to make delicious shrimp fried rice. You could always smell her cooking because she fried everything, but it was very tasty.

While we were living in Anchorage, we made it a habit to take a drive on Saturdays or Sundays, and we always stopped at McDonald's to get a hamburger for Mitch and then on to 31 Flavors where, if you bought ice cream for yourself, you got a doggie scoop for your dog. So Mitch looked forward to those drives almost as much as we did.

Jerry worked on the boat until the harbor froze over some time in December, and then he didn't work again until the end of February, when the ice in the harbor went out. During his time off, we drove everywhere the roads allowed us to drive. We went down on the Kenai Peninsula as well as to Seward, Portage Glacier, and Denali Park.

Because we weren't home a lot, we didn't make a lot of close friends, but I did make some at school. As a matter of fact, I still keep in contact with one very good friend from that time, Connie Elledge, who now lives in South Dakota.

We made some good memories during our year in Anchorage, but we were both ready to leave the big-city life after our year. In the meantime, I finished my school, and on May 9, 1980, I graduated with my master's degree. That was a very happy day for me. For my birthday on May 6, Jerry gave me a set of luggage, and then for my graduation gift, he gave me a camera, so I was all set to travel. Then he totally surprised me with a round-trip ticket home to Michigan for a visit with my family. It worked out that I arrived home on Mother's Day, and Mom was really happy with her gift that year—*me*.

CHAPTER 16

WHEN I RETURNED FROM MY Michigan vacation and with my brand-new MA degree as a reading specialist in hand, I started looking for a job. I went to the job fair at the Anchorage Hilton Hotel. From the contacts I met there, I secured an appointment to talk to a man from Lake and Peninsula School District, but when I arrived, I was told to come back the next day at half past ten or at eleven o'clock. Then he gave me the number of the room he would be in.

The next day, promptly at half past ten, I stood outside the hotel door and knocked. I didn't know what I expected, but it turned out to be his personal hotel room. And since he had been sleeping, he answered the door in his undershorts. When he saw it was me, he said, "Just a minute. I'll be right out."

Shortly he opened the door again, this time fully dressed, and we went down to the hotel coffee shop and ordered hamburgers. As we talked, I noticed his glasses were very thick and he squinted and had to get right up in my face to look at me when I talked. He picked his burger up in both hands, and when he lifted it to his mouth, he missed and smacked it into his cheek. It was pretty pathetic, but I had to bite my tongue to keep from laughing and excused myself to the restroom so I wouldn't burst into giggles.

In the end, I did have a job offer from Lake and Peninsula, but I didn't think I could work for that man because I was afraid I'd want to laugh every time I saw him. Sometime later in June, there was a job offer that came through from Yukon Koyukuk School District, whose headquarters were located in Nenana. I sent them my application, and they asked me to come up for an interview. So we hopped in the car on a Friday morning and drove the four hundred miles to Nenana from Anchorage. I went to my interview, and they offered me a contract right then and there. I was very excited because I was being hired as a reading specialist, and that just tickled me to be able to use my new degree right away.

Jerry and I went out to the car and talked it over and decided that, yes, Kaltag was someplace we wanted to go. So I signed on the proverbial dotted line, and just that easy, I was a teacher in Kaltag, Alaska.

We had planned to camp somewhere that night, but we were both so excited we just drove all the way home. We talked it over and decided we would give our apartment up at the end of July and travel around the state before we left for Kaltag. In the meantime, we got busy buying our year's supply of groceries.

We went to Safeway and filled up six heaping grocery carts. We not only filled the carts, but the shelves underneath those carts were also packed. Having shopped like this before, we pretty much knew what we would need and what we wanted, and we bought like seasoned shoppers. The bags and cartons completely filled our little VW van.

When we got home, we dumped everything out in a pile on our living room floor and took pictures of it to show the folks back home how we did things up here. Then we sorted and packed it all in sturdy boxes for shipping. What a chore that was, but I'm glad we planned ahead because that way I didn't have to buy a case of something all at once. If I only wanted five cans of a certain kind of beans, that was all I bought, and then I wouldn't have so much left over at the end of the year. Later, we discovered Prairie Market Shippers in Anchorage. They shipped things directly without having to buy in case lots, so after that, we dealt with them.

After that, we closed up the apartment and spent the rest of the summer traveling around the state, doing more sightseeing, and then we returned to Anchorage, packed up all our remaining stuff, and mailed it off to Kaltag. All that remained was for us to follow our belongings. Our old friends the Combs took us out to the airport and stayed to see us off.

It was as we were standing in line to check in when someone shouted, "Sue Nuyen?" When I turned to look, somebody started hugging me, and it turned out to be David Rhodes, a fellow

Kalamazooan. I thought it was kind of remarkable to see somebody I knew from home in the middle of the Anchorage airport, but David was working on the Alaska Pipeline in Prudhoe Bay and was on his way back up there after some time off.

Now in order to get to Kaltag, we had to fly from Anchorage to Galena on a big Alaska Airlines plane and then continue on from Galena to Kaltag in a cramped little four-seater. When we arrived in Kaltag, the pilot first buzzed the airfield before landing, and that way, the person who serviced the small airport was tipped off to the fact that passengers were arriving and they would need transportation. Buzzing the field meant flying over it really low, and then they would do one of those steep bank turns and land. Well, when the plane banked, my door flew open.

I said to the pilot as calmly as I could, "My door is open."

He answered shortly, "Oh, that's okay, we're going to land in a minute."

Well, we were banked on an angle, my side down, and as I looked at the village through the open door, I thought, *Wow! What an entrance. I'll probably fall out, and this will be my first and last trip to Kaltag.*

But we all landed safely, including the dog. There hadn't been room for the kennel on the small plane from Galena to Kaltag, so Mitch had sat on Jerry's lap for the entire trip, and he had drooled all over everything.

We arrived in Kaltag to discover a small miracle had happened! All of our boxes had arrived safely. And our house—how should I describe our house? It seems that several years before, the school had burned down, and our house was what they had used as a temporary schoolroom. We were told the building had been built originally to send to the Philippines, but unfortunately, for some unknown reason, it had ended up in Kaltag instead. Now it had been divided into two separate apartments, and we had to share the bathroom and kitchen with the tenant of the other apartment, a single woman.

Our apartment consisted of a bedroom, living room, the communal kitchen, and a big storeroom. In the entire space, there was only one window, and the nicest thing I can say about the decor is that it was ugly as sin. The bedrooms of the two apartments were next to each other, and the walls didn't go all the way to the ceiling so heat could circulate. Obviously, this didn't allow for much privacy. All the heating ducts were located in the ceiling, so in the winter, it was very cold unless you could get up high enough to get warm. At floor level, it was always freezing.

Now the fact that I would be sharing my kitchen was one of the details that had been omitted in any discussions I'd had with the school officials, and my first thought was, *We'll just go back to Anchorage.* But all our earthly possessions were already there and there we were with this woman we didn't even know and now they were telling us we would be sharing a house with her. I was not happy!

Aside from the actual living arrangement, the apartment itself was a pretty pathetic place. The door was painted a bright orange, and the lone window was located in the living room so close to the wood-burning stove you couldn't even sit in front of it to enjoy the view because it got too hot. The whole situation was pretty depressing.

In the end, we did stay, and I did learn to like it there. I had a good feeling about the village, and I came to like the people of Kaltag very much. They were Athabascan Indians, and the woman we shared the apartment with was African American, and so for a while, I was the only white woman in town. I just fell in love with the people, and I still, to this day, keep in touch with many of them.

It was a very small village of about two hundred people, and there weren't even a hundred students in the whole K-12 school. As the reading specialist, I taught everything from first grade through twelfth, and I held classes as well as offered one-on-one sessions with those students who needed extra help.

I had my own little office, and I loved it. It was a beautiful office in a brand-new school building, and the door was labeled with a sign in big letters announcing Nurse. There wasn't a nurse in the whole town, let alone one at the school, so that became my office. I had my own bathroom and windows that overlooked the Yukon River. It was a lovely space where I worked comfortably, one-on-one with my students. I also had a reading lab set up in the library where, at different times of the day, I taught seventh through twelfth graders.

The principal supervised the school from a chair behind his desk and rarely ever left his office to see anything for himself. But I will say this for him, he stood behind his teachers and made sure they had whatever support they needed.

During my first month, I had a run-in with one of the high school boys, and he called me a rather nasty name. I had heard the word before, but I had never had it applied to me, and I was just crushed. I went home and told Jerry about it. Later I found out that Jerry knew this student's parents, so he went over to their house and told them what the boy had said to me, and they were irate to think their son had done such a thing. The next day, the student apologized to me, and in the end, he turned out to be one of my favorite students. I still see him occasionally, and I am still in touch with his sisters, who were also students of mine.

I made some really good friends in Kaltag, and I always had something to do. I got involved in the women's club, which met every Wednesday night. I seemed to fit right in, and they liked me; it was a nice place to be. Jerry enjoyed our time in Kaltag. There were a lot of things for him to do there, and he got involved with the men of the village and went hunting and fishing with them. They taught him a lot, and he respected them.

Kaltag was just a neat place to live in, plus there were some really nice people there that I enjoyed getting to know. In fact, one of my very good friends from that village, Chele Bifelt, now works in Fairbanks, so I still am in contact with her.

I remember that, on our first Thanksgiving in Kaltag, we cooked a big turkey and invited several of the teachers over for dinner. There was a lot of snow that year, and huge drifts had accumulated because of the fierce winds that had been blowing. I remember Jerry and two of the other teachers climbed up on the roof of the building next door to our house and jumped off into the snowbank. It took them a long time to climb out, but they had a good time.

I remember one time in the middle of January when we had some really weird weather; it rained, and then everything froze over. When I stepped outside one morning to go to the school, which was right across the boardwalk from our house, I fell down on the ice and slid straight down the hill. I went a long way before I was finally able to stop, and then I had to crawl on my hands and knees to get back up the hill because I couldn't stand up on the ice; it was too thick and slippery.

We lived right on the Yukon River, and stepping out our side door put us right on the banks of the river. It was a lovely setting, and it was really too bad that we didn't have a window overlooking that view. Jerry built a bench there on the bank, and we had a cooking kit out there. It was beautiful and serene, and we ate many pleasant dinners out there.

In Kaltag, as in Savoonga, there was only one phone, and that was at the city offices. There was no public Laundromat in the village, but there was one automatic washer at the school. Everybody else had wringer washers in their homes because the houses in Kaltag were modern enough to have running water and flush toilets. But because the electricity was so expensive, the townspeople all used a manual wringer washer. We teachers were allowed to use the washing machine at the school, and you can believe that was one luxury I took advantage of.

The school had no electric drier, so we had to wash the clothes and then lug them home and hang them up. Jerry rigged up a clotheslines in the bedroom, and we always laughed because, on wash nights, if we woke up in the night and sat up in bed, we got smacked in the face with something wet. But that was the only place we had to hang the clothes.

When some of the ladies in the village found out what I was doing, they suggested it was better to hang the clothes outside. So Jerry went to work again and fixed up a clothesline for me out in the yard. Well, have you ever tried to operate a spring type clothespin with mitts on? Trust me on this—it doesn't work! So I took my mitts off and tried to hang the wet clothes with my bare hands. Just once was all it took, and I decided I would rather put up with the bedroom clothesline jungle than freeze my fingers off.

About three hours after I had hung my clothes up outside, Jerry came in from the yard and said, "Honey, look at this." He had gone out the side door where the outside clothesline was strung and accidentally run into my Levi's Bend Over pants hanging out to dry. In his hand, he held one leg of my slacks, which had neatly broken off from the remainder of the garment still hanging on the line. My first instinct was to cry because I had very few clothes to begin with and we weren't someplace where we could just run out and replace a pair of my good teaching slacks. But then we both started to laugh at the ridiculousness of the whole situation. I mean, how many people do you know who have broken the leg of their pants off? After that experience, we joked about freeze-drying the laundry, but it was my first and last time.

From that time on, I didn't really mind hanging the wash inside, and as it turned out, as the weather got colder and drier, the nights we slept best were the nights I did laundry because it put some needed moisture in the house and that was nice.

We had a fuel oil furnace in the house, and the school supplied the fuel oil, which was great. But the furnace alone didn't keep the place warm enough, so we also had a wood-burning stove we could use, but it was hard to regulate. We either froze or cooked, but most of the time, Jerry kept a small fire going in the stove, and he always had a pot of soup simmering on top of the stove, which was a neat bonus. Jerry's soup pot never got completely empty because he kept adding more ingredients. Sometimes it was a rabbit soup, which turned into a moose soup and ended up being split pea soup. He just kept it going and added what we had on hand, so coming home for lunch was always a good surprise.

It was also in Kaltag where my friend Chele once washed her hair and then went outside. Her hair actually froze and broke off. Actually, that had happened to me too, but Chele wore hers in a ponytail, and the whole thing froze and broke off. We quickly learned never to go outside in the cold weather with anything wet that had any value to us.

As I mentioned, the water quality was horrible, and one day, Jerry took a picture of the water because we couldn't believe it and we knew nobody back home would believe it either. I had turned the water on to fill the bathtub, and it came out bright orange. The water was thick and looked like paint coming out of the faucet. My hair and just about everything I owned was permanently stained a rusty red. Once a month, I poured a vinegar rinse on my hair to take the sediment out of it. And I remember telling Mom not to send me any clothes, especially white ones. It was just awful. Everything turned orange, and I mean *everything*!

We had a white plastic pitcher we mixed our powdered milk crystals in, and that turned orange too. Orange milk was not so appetizing, so we ended up drinking a lot of what we called red junk. It was either red Kool-Aid or red Crystal Light or anything red because that covered up the awful color of the water.

I really came to feel at home in Kaltag. It was a beautiful village in a beautiful setting, and Jerry found a lot to keep him busy there. He went beaver trapping with Larry Saunders and bear hunting with Goodwin Semaken. He went moose hunting, and although he didn't get a moose, someone in his party did. We got a hindquarter of it, which fed us for quite a while. We hung the meat up in the shed because it was cold out there, and it wouldn't thaw out. Then whenever we wanted moose meat for dinner, Jerry went out and sawed off a piece, and I cooked it.

That year, the kids in the school decided they would like to attend and participate in the Festival of Native Arts, which was held every year in Fairbanks, so I was asked to be their sponsor. Fortunately, I didn't have to teach them how to do native dancing or speak and sing in their native tongue; for that, they needed somebody from the village. But they did need a sponsor from the school to chaperone them for the event, and that was where I came in.

I agreed to do it, and I also sewed a *kuspuk*, a type of native jacket, for each child. I remember thinking to myself that it was kind of ironic that they were going to a native event and here was this little old white girl sewing up their native costumes for them. Our group numbered between fifteen and twenty kids from kindergarten through twelfth grade, and some of them were pretty special to me. We had the best time when we went into town.

The Yukon-Koyokuk school district had its own airplane, a small Learjet. We couldn't all get on at once, so we had to travel in two separate groups. The pilot, Mark Krinski, flew out and picked up the first group and then went back to pick up the second batch. We stayed in town for a week at the Captain Bartlett Hotel, and not only did we perform in the Festival of Native Arts, but I was also able to take the group on several sightseeing tours.

One day, we ate lunch at the University of Alaska Fairbanks cafeteria after we had gone to the museum there. One of the younger girls, Madeline, accidentally leaned against an emergency exit door, and that set off a loud alarm bell. All the college students in the room at the time stood up and clapped for her. She was really embarrassed, and when they saw she was crying, some of them came over and told her, "We weren't making fun of you. It's just that it happens usually once a day, but it's usually one of us that does it." That explanation made her feel a little better about it anyway.

CHAPTER 17

THERE WERE SOME FUN ACTIVITIES planned for the springtime in Kaltag. The village always held a spring carnival, which included dog races and even a contest to see who could make a fire the fastest and then boil water and make tea. There was a variety of contests for both kids and adults to celebrate the long winter being over.

One of the dog races was a cheechako race. A cheechako is a greenhorn or tenderfoot. In this case, it meant someone who had never raced a dog team before. I, of course, fit that description, so they entered me in that contest. Now I was really heavy at that time, and I warned them they would need every dog in town in front of the sled to haul me around. So they rustled up a team for me, and I perched precariously on the back of the sled. Well, those dogs went about twenty feet at the most, then they all stopped still, and lay down right where they were and refused to move any further. I was mortified, but I was just too much for them to pull. I'm sure it was best for all of us because I probably would have killed myself if the dogs had continued. But they didn't, and I didn't win the race, but I did receive the red lantern award, the prize for last place.

The people of Kaltag loved to celebrate anything, so they held a lot of potlatches, which were similar to potluck suppers in the Lower 48. They celebrated for all sorts of reasons. For example, if there was a basketball team that came in from another village for a game, they held a potlatch in the visiting team's honor. Now at a potlatch, long lengths of butcher paper were spread on the floor in lieu of tables, then everyone sat on the floor in front of the paper, and food was served to you.

At the potlatches, I noticed some guests sat at separate pieces of paper, and the reason for this was explained to me this way: In Kaltag, when people died, a memorial potlatch was held for them, which was called a stick dance. If you were chosen to be dressed for the stick dance, it meant you were being dressed in memory of the person who had died. All your clothes would be taken away and burned, and you would be presented with brand-new clothing from the inside out and from the top to the bottom. Everything would be brand new. It was a very high honor to be chosen for this, and during the year in which you had been selected, you were a special person. You would sit at the special piece of paper on the floor at every potlatch, and you'd be served a special meal. Your favorite foods were selected and prepared just for you.

The person who had asked you to represent their deceased loved one would prepare the meals for you. Your food would not be what the rest of the guests were eating. So if fried chicken was your favorite thing, you'd get fried chicken and all the trimmings. Or maybe caribou was your favorite, then you'd get caribou, while the other guests ate the regular potlatch fare.

At Kaltag potlatches, everybody brought food to share, and it was passed around instead of being served buffet style. But all dishes started at the same end of the line, so if you didn't sit at the beginning of the line, there wouldn't be much left when the dishes finally got to the end. Potlatch protocol dictated that you must take some of each food. Some looked more appetizing than others, but it was very impolite not to sample everything. Sometimes I really did not want a certain food, so I always took an extra plate, and the food I really didn't like or that I didn't want to touch any of my other food went on my extra plate, which I could then take home and dispose of discreetly.

On New Year's Day, according to Kaltag custom, they did something called pass-the-blanket. Some of the villagers came door-to-door with a blanket stretched out and held by several people. When they came to your door, you were expected to toss an item of food into the blanket, like a can of something or maybe a box of pilot bread. All the collected food was taken to the community hall and cooked up, and that night, the whole town would be invited to a potlatch of all the food that had been collected that morning.

On our first year in Kaltag, we went to Nevada to spend Christmas with my whole family at my brother and sister-in-law's home in Boulder City, Nevada. When we left home, it was fifty degrees below zero. Now planes usually wouldn't fly if the temperature was forty or more degrees below; however, because it was only forty below in Galena just downriver, planes were allowed up. When we arrived in Las Vegas, it was about seventy degrees above zero, and to me, that was *hot*! We, of course, had to bring all our winter gear with us because when we flew from Kaltag to Galena and on to Anchorage, we didn't have any place to leave our heavy clothes, so we just took it all with us. We had mukluks and snow pants. We had our marten hats and mitts and boots and big jackets. Then we landed in Las Vegas, and it felt like a blast furnace, so we just lugged all our stuff around with us.

I remember starting off on a walk with Mom, and she told me I'd better grab a sweater. I said, "Mom, I don't think so. It's sixty-five degrees here."

"Well, that's a little chilly."

"Mom," I explained, "I just came from 50 below to 65 above. That's a 115-degree difference. I'll be warm enough."

She agreed.

Flying back to Alaska from Nevada was one of the scariest things I've ever done. I flew from Las Vegas to Seattle by myself because Jerry was going on to San Antonio to visit his parents. I had to go back to Kaltag because school was starting again. Well, I got to Seattle, and we were about to land when, all of a sudden, I felt the plane go straight up, and it got very quiet in the cabin. The pilot announced it was too foggy to land, but he was going to make another pass and try again. So we circled the airport one more time, and in the silence of the cabin, you could have heard a pin drop. I looked out the window, but there was nothing to see, and I knew that if we couldn't see anything, the pilot was having trouble as well. The plane made its second descent, and again, instead of landing, we ascended.

Next the pilot announced he was going to try Boeing Field for an alternative landing. My only thought was of my dad saying,

"Three strikes, and you're out." I just knew if we didn't land on that third time, we were all going to die.

Up until that point in the trip, people had been laughing and reminiscing about the fun they'd all had in Las Vegas, and we were still on vacation. But when the whole plane went quiet, it got unnerving. The minute the wheels of the plane touched down on the Boeing Field runway, a collective cheer went up from the passengers that probably was heard all the way back to Vegas.

So there we were at Boeing Field about five or ten miles from the Sea-Tac airport. The workers rolled out the portable stairs, and we stepped into the rainy, foggy day and were told they would try to get our luggage off the plane. There was no transportation in sight. We were all just standing around in the middle of the airfield in very nasty weather.

Eventually, we made it over to Sea-Tac by shuttle and our luggage was with us and I was able to make my connecting flight out. I had thought I'd be stuck in Seattle until the fog lifted, but luckily, the plane I was taking from Seattle to Anchorage was on the ground before the fog set in, and it was able to take off exactly on time. Nevertheless, that was a pretty scary incident.

I was to overnight in Anchorage since it was too late for the small planes to fly, and when I arrived, I was only too glad to have my heavy winter coat because the temperature was forty below—back to reality! I flew back to Kaltag the next day with no further mishaps.

CHAPTER 18

I GAINED A LOT OF VALUABLE knowledge from the older ladies in Kaltag. One crisp fall day, I went walking out to the airstrip with a group of those ladies. There had been a lot of reported bear sightings around the village, so when we heard a noise in the bushes, one of the ladies shared that Athabascan custom held that if you bared your breasts, it would scare the bears away. Well, I started unbuttoning my blouse because I was really scared, but the ladies started to laugh because it had obviously been a joke on me. It must have worked though because no bears came after us.

Another time I was walking to the women's club, which was held at the school, and when I got there, somebody came running into the school and said the Eskimos were coming from Unalakleet and that everybody should get off the streets. It seemed the Athabascans were scared of Eskimos because "You never know what they might do. You know how those Eskimos are." I thought they were joking that time too, but they were dead serious. They actually believed something bad would happen when the Eskimos arrived.

While I was busy learning the ropes of the village, Jerry was furthering his education also, and one of the things he learned was how to trap beavers. It was in Kaltag that I ate beaver for the first time, and I found it to be very greasy unless you parboil it in soda water first. It is definitely not my favorite kind of meat.

I also learned about stink fish. People caught fish and buried them in the sand until they "seasoned." In other words, they let the fish rot, and then they cooked and ate them. Really! If you have that kind of a death wish, why don't you just eat out of the dumpster?

Whenever we visited other homes in the village, we were always offered a cup of tea. As a teacher, I visited a lot of people not only because of my work but because I'd also made a lot of friends. It was a hospitality matter to offer each guest a cup of tea and a piece of pilot bread, which looked like a large round soda cracker with no salt on it. So I ordered in a supply of pilot bread because many people visited our home too and "when in Rome . . ."

My second year in Kaltag was not a good year for me. I thought I'd like to have my own classroom rather than continue on as the reading specialist, and they accommodated me by giving me my own room, where I taught fourth, fifth, sixth, seventh, and eighth grades. The problem was, it wasn't really a classroom since we had to meet in the library because of space limitations. The library had no windows, so to make up for that fact, my class always got to have a recess.

Despite the location, I loved this group of kids. I still think about them, and it still makes me happy. It was a wonderful class, and I was thoroughly enjoying myself. Then one day, the principal came in and told me my replacement had arrived.

"My replacement for what?" I asked.

"The teacher who's going to take over this class so you can operate as a reading specialist again."

No wonder they were so obliging when I asked for my own class; they needed an interim teacher.

Without my knowledge, the school district had recruited another teacher, so when she arrived, I went back to being the reading specialist, which I took as a demotion. Now I didn't even have a room in the school since my "new" office was located in the old school building. But I decided to make the best of it.

The old school was directly across the boardwalk from our house, but it was in pretty bad shape and needed to be fixed up, which I managed by myself. Although the whole situation left a bad taste in my mouth, I figured whatever didn't kill me would make me stronger, and I just got on with my life. I remained as a reading specialist in Kaltag for the rest of that year, and then I decided I needed to move on.

First of all, the school district office was in Nenana. During my two years in Kaltag, I only saw the superintendent once, and that was only because he was flying his own private plane from Nenana to Unalakleet to visit a friend. The weather turned bad, so he had to land in Kaltag to wait it out. I believed if a school district was going to operate a school, there should have been a little more effort and involvement on the part of the district. But what did I know?

I left on a good note though because that was the year the teachers were asked to wear their caps and gowns to the graduation ceremony and I got to wear my master's hood for the first and only time. It was kind of exciting for me. We only had two graduates that year though, so I didn't wear my ceremonial dress very long.

CHAPTER 19

E ACH YEAR IN MARCH, THE Iditarod sled dog race came right
through Kaltag, and that was a really exciting event. Now one
year when we lived in Savoonga, we went over to Nome to see
the end of the Iditarod. When we lived in Anchorage, we had seen
the starting point. Now in Kaltag, we got to experience the middle
of it, so I felt like I had now seen the whole race. It was really fun to
see the sleds go through, and they were spread out for days at a time.

It happened that during my first year in Kaltag, the day the
mushers came through was the day I was leaving with my students
for the Festival of Native Arts in Fairbanks. So we only got to see
a couple of the mushers come in, but they were big names in the
Iditarod race. One of them was Susan Butcher, and the other was
Rick Swenson. Both had won the race several times.

While our plane was in the air, the pilot flew on a route down
the Yukon River, which was the path the Iditarod racers followed,
and could see them coming downriver from Galena. They were
stretched out for miles, and we saw them all the way from Kaltag to
Ruby, a good two-hundred-mile stretch. It was exciting to see.

During my time in Kaltag, I was on several educational com-
mittees, and I frequently had to fly into Nenana to attend meetings,
so Mark Krinski flew out to pick me up. If there were teachers in
other school district villages flying at the same time, Mark would
pick me up first and then work back because Kaltag was the furthest
village away from the district offices.

The first time I went in, I sat in the back seat and couldn't see
too much, but the next time, I got to sit up front as the copilot.
We were flying along, and he said, "We gotta stop in Galena for gas
because we're almost out." So first we landed in Nulato to pick up
a passenger, but there was no one there, so we took off for Galena
to gas up. In the meantime, Mark called Nulato to report there had

been no passengers and learned that the teacher was now ready, so we had to double back to Nulato.

It wasn't a very nice day for flying, and visibility was low, so we couldn't pick out landmarks. My job as copilot was to spot places where we could land in an emergency. Of course, Mark hadn't told me that, but that was exactly what I was trying to do. Better to be safe than sorry! So we flew back to Nulato, and they had a really horrible little airport. You had to land and go uphill, and the wheels touched down right on the bank of the river. Pretty scary for me, but I wasn't the pilot after all.

So on the way back to Nulato, Mark looked over at me and asked, "Hey, do you know where we are?"

I nearly came unglued. Of course, I didn't know where we were. I was scared to death, and I guess he must have realized that, so he said, "No problem. I know where we are."

I think he was joking around, but I didn't find it too funny. We picked up the Nulato teacher and headed to our next stop, which was Tanana, and picked up a couple of teachers there.

Well, we were flying right along, but as I glanced over at Mark, he appeared to be asleep, or at least doing a good job of faking it. I couldn't believe it. Now I was really scared, but I didn't want him to know that I was such a big chicken, so I thought, *I'll just watch the control panel, and if anything starts flickering and fluttering and lights come on or numbers go up and down, I'll wake him up.*

That lasted for about two minutes until I realized I was a nervous wreck. I couldn't stand it anymore, so I shouted, "Hey, wake up! You're supposed to be flying this plane, not sleeping."

He said calmly, "It's okay. I have it on automatic pilot."

"I don't care what it's on. I think it would be better if the pilot stayed awake."

The rest of the trip was uneventful, but on the way back, there was a problem with the plane. One of the engines quit just as we were ready to land in Tanana, so that was kind of scary. I don't know what I was thinking, but I should have just gotten out of the plane right then because I was a nervous wreck. The river was frozen over, and I could have walked on home to Kaltag. But I didn't, and in the end, I did get home safely.

Airplane experiences like that are terrifying to me. If a plane goes down over the Alaskan wilderness, there's nothing around and not much chance of it being found. It's just miles and miles and miles of nothing but tundra and river and trees.

I remember another time when Jerry and I decided to go into Anchorage just for a change of scenery. Again, the plane was a small Learjet, and during the trip, the pilot pointed out the remains of several different plane wrecks on the pass we flew over. He would say, "If you look out your right window, there's a plane over there, and then out your left window there's another."

I could have done quite nicely without hearing about all that wreckage. And we knew he wasn't just making up stories as the pilots would do sometimes for tourists because we could actually see the downed planes.

Once, the school district held an in-service, and they flew all the teachers to Fairbanks for three days. We landed in Fairbanks at a little airport (it's no longer in existence today). It had a very short runway, and it was located right on the banks of the Tanana River. I hated that. Come to think of it, I hated most things about flying in bush planes. I'm still not too thrilled with it and don't do it much anymore.

CHAPTER 20

THE PEOPLE OF KALTAG WERE allowed to fly to Galena to the air force base there and bowl or see a movie or eat in a restaurant, a real restaurant. That was quite a treat since there were no restaurants in Kaltag, and Jerry and I took advantage of that a couple of times.

One time, some people that I had met at an in-service for the school district came down from Koyokuk on snow machines to Kaltag, and that was fun. They were from Michigan, and they stayed with us for the weekend.

I loved to meet people from home. At one of the school district in-services, I met a gal who was teaching in Minto, and she told me she was from Michigan. I asked where, and she said, "You've probably never heard of it. I'm from Plainwell." Well, it just happens that Plainwell is ten miles north of Kalamazoo.

In further conversations, I learned I had graduated from high school with this girl's older sister. Her family had lived in Kalamazoo at that time, but this girl was younger, and by the time she entered high school, her parents had moved to Plainwell. She also told me her parents had moved again and now lived in a duplex in the same subdivision my mom and dad lived in. I was always learning what a really small world we lived in—even in Alaska.

Going to the post office to collect the mail was always a big event in Kaltag, and I was excited when my birthday came around because that meant I would be getting more mail than normal, so I was looking forward to that. Unfortunately, the postmistress's husband died, and the post office was closed for three days over my birthday, so I had to wait to get any mail at all.

A funeral in Kaltag was a totally new experience for me. The whole village was expected to gather at the home of the deceased, and assuming it would be similar to funerals back home, Jerry and

I joined the others at the postmistress's home. When we arrived, the dead man was lying on an old wooden pallet in the middle of the room. All the chairs were arranged in a circle around him, and people were talking and laughing and joking. I thought it quite strange and disrespectful to the man and his family.

We were served tea and smoked salmon, and then they brought out card tables and set them up and proceeded to start gambling. They played pan, which is short for panguingue, but I never quite caught on to how it was played.

When I asked someone what was happening, I was told it was the custom to keep the deceased company. Before the burial, the dead person was never to be left alone, so whenever there was a death, it was time to party.

Whenever there was a death by drowning, all the old men in the village would go out to sit on the banks of the river on benches and watch for the body to float by. Most of the time, that didn't happen. The river usually took people but didn't give them back up and they'd be lost forever. It seemed like a lot of people drowned in the river while we lived there. When that happened, alcohol was usually involved, and there was a lot of alcohol abuse—not just in Kaltag, but in other villages as well.

I really did like Kaltag; it was just my job there I didn't care for. It was a nice place to live in, but when it was time to go, I had no regrets. We packed up all our belongings and left them with John Lyle, a friend and fellow teacher who was staying in the village. He promised to ship them to us wherever we ended up following a summer on our boat.

PART IV

THE OBSERVER

I N 1980 WE HAD VISITED Wrangell, Alaska, and checked out all the beautiful boats in that picturesque harbor. That was when we started talking about buying a boat of our own. We had seen pictures in a magazine story of a new style of boat called a Nordic Tug, and it was only in the thinking stages at that time. Jerry really liked the look of it, so we talked it over and decided it was something we'd like to try.

On the way back from Christmas vacation in Boulder City, Nevada, Jerry stopped off in Seattle and paid a visit to Woodenville, Washington, where production of the Nordic Tugs was just beginning to get underway. He ordered one for us in blue and white, and we were given hull number 1, which they told us was a very great distinction and meant it was the very first Nordic Tug ever built.

The boat was ready for us to take possession of when school let out following my first year of teaching in Kaltag in 1981. So we packed up and flew down to Seattle to begin our new adventure, and Mitch went with us. We rented a car and tried to find a motel room for the night, but we couldn't find one that would let us have a dog in the room. Finally, in desperation, we went into the lobby of one of the last motels we saw, and when they said "No pets allowed," I just started to cry. I must have looked pretty pitiful because they relented and allowed us to have a room. After that time, Jerry always sent me in to rent motel rooms because he knew that if I cried, I'd get my way.

The next day, the boat was launched into the water, and from then on, we could stay on it, so we moved into our new summer home. We were tied up in Kenmore, Washington, on Lake Washington, and before we could leave, we had to outfit our boat.

Since there was nothing on it, we started from scratch with dishes and curtains and sheets and blankets and all the necessities you would need in a home. We also had to stock the kitchen (galley) with food. Now this was a pretty big boat. It was thirty feet long and had a stateroom, a head, a pilothouse, and a galley with a salon (living room) plus a back deck. It was just as cute as could be and reminded me of the pictures of Little Toot I remembered from a childhood book. We named our boat *The Observer*.

Once *The Observer* was outfitted, we had to stay in the Seattle area until we had enough hours on the engine before starting our trip back to Alaska. So we stayed in Kenmore for about three weeks, and during that time, my mom and dad, who had driven their motorhome across the country from Michigan to Wenatchee, Washington, to visit my Aunt Rose and Uncle Chuck, drove over to Seattle to see our new toy. We all stayed on the boat and had a good time visiting.

We had a grill on the back deck, so we grilled supper out almost every night, and while he waited for the grill to heat up, Jerry jumped off the deck for a predinner swim. We saw all of Lake Washington that summer while putting miles on our engine. We also found a canal through to Lake Union right next door to it, so we explored that too. We tied up at many different public docks to check out the towns, and no matter where we went, people were really interested in our boat. Everybody who came by wanted to see the inside. I felt like I was on display, but it was really fun to show off our new toy.

We had a cute little wooden skiff tied behind the boat, and once when we were tied up in Lake Union at a public dock, Jerry took the skiff out and was having a good time rowing around. He tied the skiff to a buoy to take a swim, and while he was swimming, the harbor police approached and asked what he was doing. It seemed that tying up to a buoy was illegal, so they asked to see his driver's license, which he showed them. It read, "Jerry Henning, Kaltag, Alaska," without even a PO box number. So then they came over to our boat to look it over and asked to see my driver's license, and I complied. My license read, "Suzanne Henning, General Delivery, Kaltag, Alaska." Because there was no street address on my license either, they assumed we were transients.

Well, I got really mad! Here I had a good-paying job, we had just bought this expensive boat, and they had the nerve to be telling us we were vagrants simply because our driver's licenses carried a general delivery address.

No matter how we tried, we couldn't seem to make them understand that was how we received our mail. There weren't even any mailboxes in Kaltag. People just went over to the postmistress's house, and she handed out the mail. After some thorough checking, the harbor police finally set us free, but the incident left a blot on an otherwise idyllic summer.

CHAPTER 22

THE BALLARD LOCKS IN SEATTLE connect Lake Washington and Lake Union to the Pacific Ocean, and in order to get from those two lakes into Elliott Sound, you must pass through the locks. Now *The Observer* was built in Woodenville, which is situated at the very upper tip of Lake Washington, so we had to navigate down Lake Washington into Lake Union and then into the Ballard Locks.

Passage through the locks was really quite an event. Only one boat was allowed in at a time. It was tied up, and the entry gate was closed. Then the opposite gate was raised, and depending on which way you were traveling, water either flowed in or out to raise or lower the boat. For us to enter the Pacific Ocean from the locks, we had to be lower. So we entered the first lock, and the gate closed behind us. Some of the water was drained out, and as it drained, the gate to the next lock opened. In all, there were three separate chambers we had to go through, and in each one, the process was repeated. After the third lock, the boat was at sea level, and we could enter the Pacific Ocean.

As we approached the Ballard Locks, we had to pass underneath the Aurora Street Bridge, and when we got there, it looked like a regular policeman's ball. There were police all over the place both on the bridge and in boats underneath it. It seemed there was a man on the bridge, and he was threatening to jump off.

The authorities weren't sure they should let us through, but they finally did, and when we passed under the bridge, we looked up and could see the guy just hanging up there. I thought it was pretty scary, but the next day, the newspaper reported the man hadn't jumped; the police had arrested him.

Well, we entered the Pacific without further incident, but we still needed to get more hours on the engine to ensure a smooth trip back to Alaska. So after we passed through the locks, we decided to tootle around the San Juan Islands off the coast of Washington and then make our way down to Tacoma. So that was what we did, and we also explored Elliott Bay as well as the little islands of Paulsbo and Whidbey. We had a grand time.

In each of those little island towns, there was a public dock. We tied up and restocked our pantry and water supplies and walked around the town to see the local sights. I remember, in one of the towns, we decided to put a leash on Mitch and take him with us for a walk. When we found a store we wanted to check out, Jerry tied Mitch to a garbage can, but while we were in the store, something spooked the dog, and he took off running with the garbage can clattering along behind him. He went up and down several streets before we finally caught up with him, and people were coming out of their houses to see what all the noise was. This happened shortly after our vagrancy problem with the police, and Jerry wasn't looking forward to another confrontation. He whizzed us back to the boat, and we left in a hurry.

I'm sure we saw all the towns up and down that part of the coast, and we had a good time doing it. At last, way down at the end of Elliott Bay, we came into Tacoma and made a call to Earl and Muriel Tumbloo, who were visiting her family. They came over and spent a day on the boat with us and brought their little daughter Inaay.

Soon it was time to go back through the locks again to Lake Washington. Jerry said we finally had enough time on the engine, so we took her back to have the final checks done. The boat passed all its checkpoints with flying colors, so we headed out to open water on our maiden voyage home to Alaska.

CHAPTER 23

W E LEFT IN THE AFTERNOON of a lazy summer day about midway through July. It was night when we got to the first Narrows, which was a passageway into Bellingham, Washington. There seemed to be a lot of traffic, and I remember it was a harrowing experience for both of us since it was also the first time we had navigated in unprotected seas. So we tied up at Bellingham for a day while we recuperated from that ordeal.

The next day, we left to make our way through the San Juan Islands and into British Columbia. We stopped at a place called Nanaimo, British Columbia, where we were required to go through customs. From there, we had to pass through some more Narrows. This time there were whirlpools in the water, and I'd never seen anything like this before. I had to stand on the back deck to make sure that everything was okay and we weren't going to smash into the rocks. I could look right down into those whirlpools and actually see all the way down to the bottom of the ocean. It was as if the world had opened up, and it was pretty scary.

Once through the Narrows, we anchored up at the next little town and spent the night. Each time we anchored up, we hopped in our skiff and rowed to shore to check the area out. We always tried to find secluded, bosky little coves to anchor in because they offered more privacy, and it felt a little more secure to us.

We continued on up the Inside Passage so as not to be on the open ocean, and the trip was beautiful. We passed by little towns, and I remember once we came to a place called God's Pocket. We could find the names of these places by looking on our sea charts, which we had invested in to get ourselves home. We spent about three nights in God's Pocket because the weather was really nasty, foggy, and cold. There was a buoy floating a little distance from us, and we heard it making strange moaning noises. It was a forlorn, lonely sound, and with the added howls of wolves in the darkness, it was enough to raise goose bumps on our arms. From there, we had to cross Queen Charlotte's Strait, which was open to the ocean, and with a small boat like ours, bad weather sailing was not a good idea.

While we waited for the weather to calm, we went on the skiff to an island that was affording us protection from the open ocean to do some beachcombing. Once we got there, we walked to the ocean side of the island, and we found a big glass ball, possibly a Japanese fishing float. We were happy with our treasure.

There were several other boats anchored in God's Pocket, also waiting out the weather. Finally, the day came when we thought we could make it safely through Queen Charlotte's Strait, so we set out in beautiful sunshine. We were about halfway into the strait when the wind began to whip us around, and a horrible storm came up. I can tell you without a doubt that this was the time I was the most scared I had ever been in my entire life. The only thing I could think of to do was to sing the old hymn "God Will Take Care of You" over and over.

I was so scared I couldn't move. Jerry was at the wheel, I was sitting on the other seat in the wheelhouse, and I literally could not move a muscle. Things were flying everywhere, and this was after we had secured or taken down and put away everything we possibly could. But still things were flying every which way.

Now we had to move the boat crosswise of the water trough, which meant the waves were hitting the sides of the boat and we had to go real fast. Then when the next wave came, we had to turn the boat really fast and put the bow into the waves so we wouldn't capsize. Even so, there were times when I was looking out a side window in the wheelhouse and all I could see was the green of the ocean water and no sky at all because the boat was on its side.

So there we were in the middle of that storm. The dog was under the table, cringing in fear because the boat was just rocking and rolling. Then Jerry announced, "'M 'ungry." I told him if he wanted something to eat that badly, he'd have to go get it himself because I wasn't leaving that seat. Actually, I could have used the bathroom about then, but there was no way I was even getting up for that. Oh, how I wished I had a seatbelt!

While we were making the crossing, a big Alaska State Ferry approached us, going the other way. *Well,* I thought, *at least if I'm going to die out here, there will be some Alaskans around to pick up my body, and I won't die in a foreign country alone.*

Good news! We did make it across and through the storm very carefully and very slowly. We made it to the other side where we came to a town called Bella Koola. I remember pulling up to that dock to get some fuel. Now one of my jobs was to jump off the boat and wrap the rope around the cleat. So I jumped off, but my legs were just like rubber, and I fell down. I guess I was still so scared that they wouldn't hold me, and I fell smack, right on my face. That was when I decided that if we ever had to make that particular crossing again, I wanted somebody else to do it because I would never do that again.

CHAPTER 24

THE NEXT DAY, THE SUN was shining, and it was beautiful again. It was just the most pleasant day, and you never would have suspected how hair-raising the weather had been the day before because the water was as smooth as glass. We were just tootling along in the middle of the ocean, and it was lovely.

We continued up the Inside Passage, and that night, we stopped in a little town whose name I've forgotten. What I do remember is that it looked like a quaint little Western town, the kind that reminded you of Matt Dillon and Wyatt Earp. We tied up at the public harbor and prepared to do some laundry. To save time, I was to take the laundry, and Jerry would do some other errands. Well, while I was loading the washing machine, the biggest, hairiest black spider I've ever seen in my life crawled out from under one of the other machines, and I just stood there, petrified. I was afraid that spider would crawl into our clothes.

Finally, it crawled back under another machine, and I hurried as fast as I could to get out of there. We stayed in that town for another day to get groceries and fuel and to rest up for the next leg of our voyage, but I was constantly on the lookout for that spider or any of its relatives.

Some nights later, we anchored up in another beautiful little cove that offered some protection and peace from the weather, which had once again turned terrible. The wind was blowing, so we took turns staying up during the night, taking alternate watches to make sure the anchor didn't drag because if that happened, we would end up on the rocks. We dropped two anchors, one in the bow and one in the stern, and then we threw one over the very back to steady us a little more. Nevertheless, it was still pretty scary and miserable, and it was a good thing we kept watch because during Jerry's shift, the boat did move. But he was able to correct it in time.

Several times when we anchored in different coves in Canada, there were anchoring buoys specifically for boats to anchor up to. That was a relief because we didn't have to stay up all night worrying if our anchor was going to drag.

I just can't begin to describe the tranquility of those little places out in the middle of nowhere. There were lots of interesting locations to stop and check out, and we met a lot of really nice people who were taking boats either up or down the Inside Passage from Seattle to Alaska or some point along the way.

Jerry and I took turns steering the boat. He would steer for an hour, and then he'd rest. Then I would take the wheel, and I found it was really kind of fun as well as interesting. I remember one day during my turn the ocean was really calm, and Jerry decided to go out on the deck for a little nap.

I was just tootling along, and I thought to myself, *The water is so pretty and so still. It looks just like a mirror. I think I'll mess it up a little.* So I turned the boat in a huge circle.

Well, Jerry came tearing in off the deck, hell-bent for leather. "What in the hell is going on?"

I was just laughing and told him, "I just wanted to upset the water a little so I could make sure we'd been here."

When it was Jerry's turn to take the wheel again, I went out on the deck to sunbathe. I didn't have a bathing suit, so I took my shirt off. I was relaxing on the deck in my birthday suit, and the sun felt so warm and nice I eventually fell asleep. All too soon, my hour was up, and Jerry called that it was my turn to steer again. So reluctantly I got up, dressed, and went inside and told him about my nude sunbathing.

Without missing a beat, he said, "That must be why that last boat came so close. I wondered why they kept getting over closer to us. They must have been able to see you."

I was mortified, and he had me believing it until he started to laugh and I knew he'd been kidding.

At night, especially when we were anchored in a cove and there was no wind, we could hear the gentle slap, slap, slap of the waves.

On many nights, we were rocked to sleep that way. I absolutely loved it, and it seemed the perfect way to live.

We stopped at Prince Rupert, British Columbia, and there were lots of boats tied up there. We stayed for a couple of days and caught up on some laundry and did some grocery shopping. We also passed through another customs checkpoint and then headed out into Dixon Entrance, where we entered Alaskan waters for the first time on our trip.

That night, we anchored up in a cove where a couple of other boats were already anchored. It turned out the boats belonged to some fishermen, and they gave us all sorts of fish. They came aboard *The Observer* for coffee, and then we went aboard one of their boats. It seemed a neighborly thing to do, and we enjoyed visiting with them.

Next stop was Ketchikan, Alaska. As we approached the harbor, we noticed a man fishing off some rocks. Suddenly, he seemed to get really angry and started yelling at us about leaving a wake and disturbing the fish, so we just passed right on by and left him alone. A little further on, we anchored instead in a little cove where nobody objected to us being there.

We passed lots of little towns along the way, towns accessible only by boat or plane since there were no roads leading into them. Summer was waning when we took the back channel into Wrangell, and since we had once lived in Wrangell, it felt like we were home again. We stayed there for a few days, toying with the idea of leaving our boat there for the winter, but in the end, we didn't. Jerry felt the boat needed to be hauled out of the water for the winter, but for that, we needed a hoist, and there was no hoist in Wrangell or the neighboring town of Petersburg. In fact, the only hoists in all of southeast Alaska were in Sitka and Juneau.

So we traveled on to Petersburg, where my friend Celia Carlson and her husband, Dave, lived. They invited us over for dinner, and then I had to fly home because it was almost time for school to start again and I had to get back to work. I left Jerry on the boat, and he took it by himself from Petersburg to Juneau, where it was dry-docked for the winter in Auke Bay. Then Jerry flew home to Kaltag.

The winter snows in southeast Alaska could be very wet and heavy, and Jerry said that even if the boat was in dry dock, if the snow got too heavy, it could crack the hull. Our hull was fiberglass, so he worried about that for most of the winter. But the marina workers did a fine job of cleaning the snow off, and *The Observer* wintered very well.

In the meantime, we dreamed of the next summer and could hardly wait until we could get back to Juneau and put out to sea once more. Jerry spent part of his time writing an article for a boat magazine called *The Trawler*. They were interested in this new type of vessel and wanted all the facts. That kept him busy, and he enjoyed doing it.

CHAPTER 25

A T LAST, SUMMER CAME, AND school was out again. We could get back to the seagoing life we had learned to love and had longed for during the cold months of the Arctic winter. I had quit my job, packed everything up, and flew down to Juneau. Jerry was already there and had our boat in the water. He picked me up at the airport and took me right out to *The Observer*, and I was so happy to be back on that boat. It seemed like home to me.

The next day, because the sun was out, which was unusual in southeast Alaska because it was a rainforest, we decided to take the boat out and have a leisurely trip around the harbor and have a picnic on board. Well, we were just tootling around in an uncharted area when we got stuck. We ran aground, and the tide was going out. The boat was on a rock, and there was no way we could move. As the tide continued ebbing, *The Observer* began to tip, so Jerry unhooked our shiny, sturdy, new aluminum skiff and shoved it underneath the boat to hold it up. Then he placed a Mayday call to the Coast Guard, and when they arrived, they told us we, sure enough, had landed on a rock that was uncharted. The rock is now known as Henning's Rock.

The Coast Guard officials also told us there wasn't much they could do for us, but they checked everything out and pronounced us "okay." And then helped shore us up with a few more logs and left one of their people on the boat to wait with us until the tide came back in.

Jerry was able to get off the boat, but it was too much of a drop for me, so I was trapped on the boat for at least twelve hours along with the man from the Coast Guard and Mitch. Jerry came back after doing some exploring. Sure enough, that evening, the water came up again, and as soon as it was high enough, we floated right off that rock. Luckily, we hadn't sustained any structural damage, and we just floated away into the sunset.

We were able to take our time, so we went over to Sitka to visit friends and then on to Tenakee Springs, where we spent several days. That was such a pretty spot, and I remember when we tied up at the public dock, there was a boat next to us belonging to a floating dentist. He had his office right on his boat, so Jerry took advantage of the situation and made an appointment to have his teeth cleaned and checked.

We also stopped at the picturesque town of Baranof Warm Springs. It was located on Baranof Island directly across from Sitka, and the only way to get there was by boat or plane. I had never been there before, and I fell in love with the place. There were bathhouses with warm springs piped in and big tanks to bathe in that were even closer to the source of the water, and the temperature of the water increased as we got closer. We chose the tank farthest away, and it was marvelous. The water was so warm. There was no time limit on how long we could stay, so we enjoyed it for quite a while before we climbed out and dried off, and then we hiked all around the area, shooting pictures.

While we were in Baranof Springs, a big yacht tied up next to us, and a very young-looking couple got off. It turned out they were the captain and his wife for the owners of the boat and were taking it from Seattle to Juneau because the owners were flying to Juneau and then planned to travel by yacht around Alaska for a month.

They were a very nice young couple and invited us to come aboard for a tour of the yacht. It was a huge boat and made *The Observer* look like a toy in a bathtub. There were four staterooms, two heads, and a huge galley and salon. It was the most incredible boat I had ever seen; there were big decks for relaxing. We decided it was way too big for us, but it was nice to see how the other half lived.

We traveled back to Sitka and anchored up in a bay just outside of town near the ferry terminal. It was a beautiful day, and Jerry decided to take Mitch and go ashore, while I would stay on the boat and read and relax in the warm sun. The two of them left midmorning, and when they hadn't come back by six that evening, I was beginning to get a little worried. I made up my mind that if they weren't back by nine o'clock, I was going to have to put in a Mayday call.

About eight-thirty, they came rowing back, and what a story they had! They had been walking around on a beach near Sitka and were back away from the water when the dog scared up a bear. Well, it scared the pants off Jerry, and he scrambled up a tree. The dog took off barking into the woods, and when Mitch didn't come back, Jerry figured he was dead.

After a long time, to make sure the bear was well out of range, Jerry climbed down the tree and whistled for the dog, hoping against hope that somehow Mitch had survived the ordeal. He searched for quite a while and didn't find anything, so he headed back to the shore where he'd beached the skiff, and then he heard a whimper. He did a little investigating and discovered Mitch, who had fallen into a big underground pool of water, where the bear had apparently chased him. The dog absolutely hated water, but that was where he was, and it had kept him safe. He was overjoyed to see his best pal, Jerry.

Jerry fished Mitch out of the water and deposited him safely into the skiff and headed back for our boat. Jerry told me later he figured both he and the dog were as good as dead, and that was the last time Jerry ever went ashore without taking his gun with him.

CHAPTER 26

WHILE WE WERE TIED UP in Sitka, we visited all our old friends. Coke Oines, who had been our next-door neighbor when we lived there, brought her two boys down. Jerry took them for a ride in the skiff, and then we all went to dinner. We also had a chance to visit with Fran Conger over dinner, and we got to see Ben Forbes too. We tootled around the harbor in our boat and finally ended up back in Wrangell.

After careful discussion, we made the decision to leave our boat in Wrangell for the winter, so we took a slip at Shoemaker Harbor, a brand-new harbor, about five miles out of town. We stayed there for the rest of the summer and enjoyed every minute of it. We even made some new good friends, Bob and Holly Bashlear, who offered to take care of our boat during the winter. We ended up keeping our boat docked in Wrangell at Shoemaker for the rest of the time we owned it.

Our car was already in Wrangell since we had brought it there by ferry, so we were able to explore all the passable roads. We hiked all the paths we could find and took the boat out to different coves to anchor and explore those also.

One of the islands we anchored up at had a dock. The logging company that had once headquartered there was long gone, and it was now deserted. We had a lot of fun investigating the logging roads that crisscrossed the island.

We did some fishing, and I caught something that was just horrendous. It looked like a snake. I still don't know what it was, but Jerry snapped a picture of it. Jerry caught what was called a skate. It was the biggest, ugliest fish I'd ever seen. It was so big it actually pulled our boat around until Jerry removed the hook and let it escape.

Our slip at Shoemaker Harbor was right next to a shrimper, and he went out shrimping every day. He always shared his bounty with us, so we had all the shrimp we could possibly eat. And these weren't the tiny little things you get out of a can; they were three-biters. I thought I'd died and gone to shrimp heaven. We had shrimp and crab or some kind of fresh fish every night of the week.

That was also the year some of the tourists who came in on the ferry would sometimes pull their campers up and park in the parking lot of the harbor to camp. We met the nicest people from Georgia, two couples who were traveling together. We got to know them quite well and took them out on our boat a few times. I still stay in touch with them.

The Bashlears had a sailboat called *Rose*, and they also had a homestead at Olive Cove about twenty miles southeast of Wrangell where they were building a house. They invited us out, so we anchored up in the cove and stayed for a few days and helped them work on their house. It was situated on a small island, so we hiked around the island when work was finished for the day. I remember Holly and I staged some serious cribbage tournaments with "jewels" as prizes. The jewels were big, fake, and plastic, and whoever won took temporary possession of them. We had some good times.

Jerry and I played a lot of cribbage also. Our stakes, though, were not for plastic jewels or even money but to see who would empty the honey bucket on the boat. So whoever lost the evening's match won the honor of that unpleasant task. That was a very nasty chore that neither of us enjoyed, so it was cutthroat cribbage at its best. Most of the time, Jerry won since he was the better player, but on those rare occasions I won, I loved to rub salt in his wounds and laugh at him.

Wrangell held a big annual logging show and festival around the Fourth of July, complete with a parade through the middle of town, so of course, we celebrated right along with the locals since we felt like it was our town too.

Jerry built a sail for our skiff that summer so we could sail around and visit friends, and we had fun doing that. In the harbor, there were a lot of people who lived on their boats, so we always had neighbors, and we met a lot of nice people that way. It was a relaxed, laid-back way of life, and we took advantage of it and lived life to its fullest measure that summer.

We wandered over to Petersburg a couple of times to visit the Carlsons. Petersburg was an interesting town in that its Norwegian roots were reflected in the architecture of the homes, which all seemed to have a charming Scandinavian look to them.

But most of our time was spent in and around Wrangell. It was a safe, pleasant place to be, and even the weather, which was usually very wet, cooperated that summer. We enjoyed warm days and cool night breezes. Sometimes we'd go down to the ferry dock and watch the big boats come in, and one time, we were surprised to see John Lyle from Kaltag get off the boat. It was a treat to see someone we knew.

I had lots of time to read and stitch that summer, and I did plenty of both. Jerry was always busy working on something for the boat. He tied a net so we could hang it in the wheelhouse behind the steering wheel to store our charts. And then he tied another net and fastened it across the V part of our berth to hold extra clothes and shoes so they would be out of the way.

We did have a clothes locker, which was like a closet, and there was drawer storage as well as storage space underneath the berth and also under the seats in the salon. Under the back deck was more storage space, where we kept things like the grill and tools. We had some storage places that were empty because we had so much room.

We tried our hand at crabbing that summer but without much luck. Once, a fisherman who dragged the bottom of the ocean for shrimp pulled up a sponge. I knew sponges grew in the ocean, but I had never seen a fresh one. He gave it to me for a souvenir, and I still have it.

Sometimes we went ashore to pick berries. There were lots of salmonberries and blueberries, but we found out that because it was so damp down there, there were a lot of worms and bugs in the berries. So we soaked them overnight and then skimmed the bugs off before we stored them. When I saw how many worms came out of the berries, I wouldn't eat them anymore. In the interior, where the climate is dry, we don't have that problem, and the berries are very tasty and worth the effort of picking them.

We put a lot of miles on our boat in the two summers we spent on it. Sometimes when we went into Wrangell for groceries, we took the boat in and tied up at the public boat dock because Shoemaker Harbor was several miles from town. We had a little cart we took with us, and we'd fill it up with groceries or water or fuel, whatever we needed, and trot it back down to the boat.

During that second "boat summer," I was looking for another teaching job, so every few days, I called the school district office to check on openings in Tanana because that was where we'd decided we wanted to go next. But the school board hadn't had a chance to meet because all the members were at fish camp. At last, I got the word that I had been hired and school was starting in three days.

With mixed feelings, I left Jerry on the boat and boarded a plane that would take me from Wrangell to Anchorage, where I did some last-minute shopping before starting my next adventure. Jerry stayed on the boat for another four weeks and then joined me in Tanana.

After those two relaxing summers on the boat, our lives got pretty busy, and summers were usually taken up with visiting relatives on the outside. So in 1984, after some serious discussion and with many regrets, we decided to sell our floating home to a man in Wrangell who had shown a lot of interest in it. He moved it back down to Juneau, and as far as I know, that's where it still is.

I still remember those carefree summers when we just wandered around from town to town and explored a lot of what Alaska was really like. I know we only scratched the surface, but I will always treasure those memories.

PART V
TANANA-HEALY SAGA

TANANA, ALASKA, IS LOCATED ONE hundred forty air miles northwest of Fairbanks at the confluence of the Yukon and Tanana Rivers. There are only two ways to reach the village; the first is to fly in on one of the small airlines. There is a choice of Frontier Airlines, Larry's Air Service, Warbelow's, or Wright's Flying Service. If you are really adventurous, you can charter a flight with an individual bush pilot. The flight takes between forty-five minutes and an hour depending on the size of the plane and the weather conditions. You fly over absolutely undeveloped country, and quite often, you may spot elk, bear or other wildlife. It's actually a very pretty trip at any season of the year.

The other way to reach Tanana is to take your own boat down the river, but that only works during the months the river is not frozen over. There is no organized boat service, but in your own craft, you could leave from Fairbanks, travel down the Chena River to the Tanana River until it flows into the Yukon, and you're there. Tanana is definitely a remote village.

When I accepted the position in Tanana, I was told by Bob Jackman, the school superintendent, there was only one available house to live in, and I said, "We'll take it." I knew from experience what the housing situation was like in the villages; there never seemed to be any place to live. I didn't even ask what the rent would be. I didn't care as long as we had a place to call our own.

It seemed that everyone else had passed this place up because the rent was too high at four hundred dollars a month. It was an octagonal-shaped log cabin, and I thought it was beautiful. There was just one tiny problem; the newly hired English teacher was staying in the cabin until he could find something less expensive to rent.

I figured that was okay for the time being since Jerry was still down south, closing the boat up for winter. So I stayed temporarily with two other woman teachers, Carol Jackson and Lynn Mooney, who were living in a school-owned trailer. I had to sleep on the couch. The first morning when I woke up, I stepped out onto the porch to enjoy the view of the river when suddenly I heard the most horrible caterwauling. It was awful and sounded like someone was being tortured. Now the school trailers were positioned fairly close to one another, and the noise turned out to be the teacher in the neighboring unit, David Piasecki (Pi), who was singing in his shower. Pi became one of our closest friends, but we never asked him to sing after that.

Interestingly, Pi retired a few years ago from the Healy schools, finishing his long career in Alaska, and I was invited to participate in a *This is Your Life* type of program to be a voice from his past. I remember saying something about his horrible singing, which we had teased him about all those years ago, and he identified me immediately.

I only stayed with Lynn and Carol for two days, and to make a long story short, I ended up staying with Bob Jackman and his wife, Jane. Jane was a good friend of mine and was the kindergarten teacher in town. I had known both of the Jackmans before I moved to Tanana.

Well, I stayed with them until school had started, and by the time Jerry came in, the English teacher was still living in our house. Now mind you, I was paying rent on the property, and he was living there and refused to move out. So when Jerry showed up, we paid him a visit, and Jerry said with strained politeness, "Let me put it this way. I'll help you pack. Where are your boxes?"

Well, the man was unprepared and didn't have any boxes, so Jerry went out and got boxes, and we helped him move. In a last ditch effort, the English teacher and his family approached us with a deal: maybe we could all live there together. Now you have to remember, we had just come from Kaltag, where we had shared a house with an unmarried woman, and Jerry, being a very private individual, hadn't been happy with that situation at all. Neither of us was anxious to live with a man, his wife, and their son, who was to be one of my students.

So Jerry told them emphatically, "No. It won't work."

So they moved to the other side of the log cabin, which had been divided into two halves because it had previously been used as a store. Their side didn't have a bathroom because it had been the front section of the store, but they had an outhouse, and at least, the dividing walls went all the way to the ceiling.

Finally, we moved into our house, and I thought it was absolutely gorgeous. It had four bedrooms. One of them was kind of a weird shape with the house being octagonal, so we used it as a storeroom/workroom, and it made a good shop for all of Jerry's projects. Each of the bedrooms had a huge closet, and there was a gigantic living room with built-in bookshelves and a thick, cushy carpet. The house had two full bathrooms, one off the master bedroom and one off the living room. It had a cozy kitchen with a nice dining area. The only problem was, there was no furniture.

So there we were in this beautiful home with nothing but a table and chairs and a piano. I had always wanted a piano, but that was the least of my worries now; we didn't have anything else. Eventually, the school provided some furniture for us, and we ended up with two double beds, a couch, two easy chairs, a desk, and some odds and ends. We didn't have a freezer back then, but after October, the whole village of Tanana was a freezer. Jerry built a food box on our porch, and that was where we stored our frozen goods—at least until the following April. It was really a very comfortable home, and the best part of it all was, it was located right on Front Street along the Yukon River. From our kitchen window, we could watch the river, and that was neat. I referred to it as my eye on the world.

Our house was right next door to a cute little log cabin owned by Joe and Gladys John. They were the oldest people in Tanana and very friendly. Whenever Jerry had to go away, Joe came over and told him, "Don't worry, I'll take care of your wife." Now Joe was a skinny little man, and we laughed at the thought that he could take care of me if anything went wrong. Fortunately, I didn't have any emergencies, so I didn't have to find out.

Just when we arrived in Tanana, one of the villagers, Asa Dick, died, and the village was putting on a potlatch for him, so we attended with the new English teacher and his wife. Now they were "earth people," and by that, I mean they only ate fine rice and grains and no meat. You'd soon learn in Tanana that when at a potlatch, you sat down and were served, you'd better eat what they had and never refuse anything. These people got right up with their plates and proceeded to the tables where the food was laid out and started helping themselves, which they soon found was a mistake. They were immediately told to sit down and wait to be served.

When the meat was passed, the English teacher asked what it was and then flatly refused it. That got them off on the wrong foot, and the people in the village steered clear of them after that.

A school board meeting was scheduled for the day following the potlatch. Karen Williams, a village resident that had taken a liking to the English teacher and his wife, stood up and said she was just appalled this family did not have a place to live in. She proposed the two single men teachers at the school should be living together so this family—she emphasized the word *family*—could have a regular house.

Now it so happened the two men teachers who were each living alone had been in Tanana for several years but had always paid their rent on time. Neither of them felt they should have to change their living arrangement simply because they happened to be single gentlemen. So Karen then suggested that since our house was so large, we should have them live with us.

At that point, Pi, one of the two single teachers, requested the floor and suggested to Williams, "Maybe the family should live with you. You have plenty of space." At that point, the woman got all teary-eyed and cried and carried on.

Pi, who was sitting next to me, sat back down and handed me a box of tissues and said, "Here. Just in case you want to cry too."

The meeting continued, and members of the school board questioned me as to why I "threw them out" of my house. I patiently explained that the house had been rented to me to begin with and that the English teacher's family had had first choice on the house but had refused it. I further explained that when I was hired, I had rented the house, sight unseen, and I had been paying rent since that time. I produced my check stubs to show I had already been paying rent while the other family was living there.

As it turned out, a couple of days later, the English teacher and his family packed up and left town, and not just because they didn't have a place to live but because they had come to the conclusion they were just too "citified" to fit into the Tanana lifestyle.

CHAPTER 28

ND SO BEGAN MY FIRST school year in Tanana. I was teaching fourth and fifth grades, and I was excited and anxious to get on with it. I had nine students that I absolutely loved. That class included Stephanie Swenson, Marvin Anderson, Brian Dick, Daphne Huntington, Ginger Kennedy, Amber Bowen, Cheryl Folger, George Roberts, and Kenny Woods. I couldn't have asked for a better group of kids to start out my Tanana career.

It took a while for me to learn the ins and outs of living in Tanana, but my class was real good about helping me, and they loved to come to our house to visit. One student had a really terrible home life. His parents drank pretty heavily and many times he came late to school and, his excuse, consistently, was that he'd overslept. So Jerry and I bought him an alarm clock, but later, I discovered some of the real reasons for his tardiness. Once he had to get up in the middle of the night to take his sick two-year-old brother to the clinic. He explained his parents were "passed out" and he had spent the night at the clinic and was just too tired to get up for school.

I quickly learned you couldn't hold a kid accountable for something like that. Many of the kids had almost sole responsibility for caring for their younger siblings and for worrying about where their food was going to come from.

One student, Marvin Anderson, visited us often and particularly liked to have supper with us. He was completely comfortable with us, and we enjoyed his company. I remember, that year at Christmas, he came over and helped decorate our tree, and we made it a point to have presents under the tree with his name on them. Of course, I had presents for each student in my class, but Marvin was just special to me. He always seemed to show up at about dinnertime, so I knew he was hungry, and that didn't bother me at all. I just set another place at the table for him.

Later on in the school year, the kids decided they wanted to make some money so we could do some extra things as a class. I told them, "We'll learn how to sew." So I had the girls come over to my house and taught them to use the sewing machine, and we made a quilt and raffled it off.

Two of the girls, Daphne and Amber, loved to come over to my house just to do my dishes. Of course, I never turned that down. I later found out the reason was that we had running water; they liked to play in it, so they came over a lot. And then I started inviting a different student to our home for supper on Friday nights. Jerry and I always tried to make it special. If we were serving pizza, our house became Henning Hut, and when we served hamburgers, fries, and shakes, it was known as McHenning's. The kids always seemed to have grand times sharing dinner with H and her husband.

The year we spent in that first house was great. We watched the Yukon River freeze up in the first part of October. On a clear day, we could look out our window and see the back side of Denali all the way down in Healy. It was a gorgeous sight. We watched people go by on their way to the store, and we could see who was walking and who was riding their three-wheeler. We could see just about everything, so it really was our window on the world, and that was cool.

We didn't have a washer and dryer in the house, so we had to go to the Laundromat. The Laundromat was only open certain hours, so Jerry volunteered to do the laundry since he wasn't working outside the home. He loaded up the wash, lugged it over, and proceeded to wash the clothes. That night, when I got home, he said, "I'm never doing laundry again. I was laughed right out of the place because that is woman's work."

In the villages, there was a definite dividing line between men's and women's work, and he had crossed it. He said, "I'll do everything else—clean the bathroom, change the bed, and even get the laundry ready for you and haul it down there, but you do the laundry." So I did, and from that time on, he kept his word. Every Friday, he always had it ready and hauled it over on our sled, but I did the actual washing.

That was also the year of the great lice epidemic. When I did my student teaching at Gull Road Elementary School in Kalamazoo, Michigan, we had a lice outbreak, and I had to learn what a louse sac looked like. Well, one of the girls in my room was itching and scratching, and she asked me to look at her head to see if I could see any reason for it. The minute I looked at it, I knew immediately it was lice. This girl had the most beautiful long curly hair, and it was just crawling with lice. I could see the live ones moving around among the lice sacs. I alerted her mother, who was also a teacher at the school, and she said maybe I should check the rest of the class.

On closer inspection, I found that two or three other students were also infected with lice, and when the administration learned that I knew how to check for lice, every kid in the school was sent to my room so I could check their heads for lice. There were several positives, and they were all sent home with bottles of Quell shampoo and were given explicit instructions on how to wash their hair with it. The next day, the only kid in my class was George Roberts, and he and I had a great day. Everybody else was home, trying to wash everything they owned to get rid of the lice.

It didn't take long for word to spread through the village that Suzanne Henning knew how to check for lice, and the whole village started showing up at school so I could check their heads for lice too. All day long, I had a steady stream of people, and I'd pull out the little lice sacs from their hair and put them under a microscope to show them what it was. They would leave and trudge over to the clinic to get their bottles of Quell and then home to begin the anti-dotal treatment. It seemed like the whole village was washing heads and laundry.

The first day, after checking all those heads, I dragged myself home bone-tired, and Jerry, bless his heart, knew I had had a hard day, so he had gone over to the store and bought two big steaks for our supper. Now that was quite a treat since steaks, at that time, cost about ten dollars each. The minute I was in the door, I ripped off my clothes and jumped in the shower. I'd been messing with lice all day and I just itched and I wanted to feel clean again.

While I showered, Jerry started fixing dinner. It was a lovely dinner. We sat down to eat, and my steak was done rare, just the way I liked it. As I shook salt out of the shaker onto the meat, I was instantly sick to my stomach! Those little grains of salt looked just like lice sacs, and I just couldn't force myself to take even one bite, so Jerry ended up with two steaks.

From that time on, when the kids came to school, they were not allowed to hang their coats in the closet. They kept them at their desks, but still we found more lice because the lice were able to live for a certain amount of time on the wolf ruffs that trimmed most of the coats. So after placing each coat in a plastic bag, we set them outside so the bugs would freeze.

At that time, my hair was really long, so I wore it up in a bun. Jerry said I looked like an old maid librarian. Personally, I didn't care what I looked like. I just knew my hair was not going to be dragged around because I didn't want to get lice. Eventually, we licked the lice epidemic. There were more individual episodes over the years, and I had to check more heads for lice, but it never was quite as bad as that first time because now, thanks to me, they all knew how to check for lice themselves.

CHAPTER 29

O N THAT FIRST YEAR, DAVID and Patty Bowen were going "outside" for Christmas, and they asked if we'd take care of their dogsled team for them while they were gone. Jerry said yes.

Well, had I known the work that was involved in caring for a dogsled team, I never would have agreed to it. There were only eight dogs, which really wasn't very many for a sled team, but they required a lot of attention. First of all, dogsled team dogs are not pets regardless of what you may have heard. We tied them up in our yard, and Jerry fed and watered them. When it got really cold outside, their dog food must be cooked because they had to have something hot, just like people did. The food was a mixture of water, fish heads, and fish guts mixed with regular dog food. Most people kept the dog food pot outside and cooked it over a fire out there, but we didn't have that setup, so Jerry cooked it on the stove in the house and took it out to the dogs. It stunk up—and I do mean *stunk up*—the whole place. It was gross.

Well, Christmas was coming up, and there were a couple of days when Jerry went into Fairbanks to do his Christmas shopping, so the dogs became my responsibility. I said, "Just so you know, I am not cooking for these dogs after I get home from working all day." Jerry said that was fine, and for a couple of days, I could just toss them half of a dried fish. In the village, they had what they referred to as dogfish, which they caught during the last run of the salmon. They were dried on a drying rack and stored in cribs, and they stunk to high heaven. So at feeding time, you'd just chop up a frozen fish and throw it to the dogs.

I understand now why you'd throw it to the dogs because when you went out the door with the food in your hands, it would become a feeding frenzy. The dogs would all try to grab it at once, and they ripped it apart just the way you would see a starving wild animal do it. I really didn't want to think about what would happen if the dogs were taking the food from my hand, but I managed to get through the two days by myself. I vowed right then and there I would never do that again.

The dogs were still with us on New Year's Eve, and Jerry came in from feeding them and announced, "Well, now we know why Bobo isn't eating. Bobo just had a litter of pups." The temperature was at forty below zero, so he brought the dog in and made her and the babies comfortable in the workroom, where she proceeded to have a couple more pups. In the days that followed, we discovered she liked to chew things. Jerry had laid down cardboard for her to lie on— she chewed that up. She chewed the side of the storage chest. She chewed everything in sight. We put some old towels down to make her more comfortable, and she chewed them to shreds. Everything smelled because she didn't go outside to do her business, and it was a real mess. The final pup count was seven, and as soon as it warmed up to minus twenty, Bobo and her family could go back outside. I was thankful for that.

The Bowens decided to extend their Christmas break into February, so the dogs remained our responsibility, and the pups all survived until Jerry had to go away again and I had to throw fish to them. Just at the moment I threw the fish, one of the pups was trying to get some food out of another dog's bowl. The big dogs were tied up, but the little pups were just running wild. The food thief accidentally got in the way of one of the dogs I had thrown the fish to, and the big dog bit the little dog's head off.

I said, "That is it! I will never have a dog team or take care of one for anybody else ever again in this lifetime." I was a wreck by the time the Bowens came back in February, and I told Jerry he could never ever volunteer to take care of anyone's dogs again as long as I drew breath.

Around that time, Jerry started being a dog timer. He timed the dog races that took place in the winter on the Yukon River, and he really enjoyed doing that. Fortunately, he was satisfied just timing the races and never had an interest in having a team of his own. We already had Mitch, and that was enough for us.

Many families in Tanana did have teams, and every Saturday and Sunday during the winter months, the town staged dogsled races. The racers started out on trails that run behind the town, and then as the ice on the Yukon River became covered with snow and had a smoother surface, the races were actually held on the river. The river didn't freeze flat like the small inland lakes in Michigan; it froze in big chunks that looked kind of like icy waves. The snow filled in the holes and smoothed out the surface, and it made a wonderful racecourse.

Some of the big-name dogsled mushers in Alaska lived in Tanana. Curtis Erhart and Lester Erhart, for example, were two contenders that had won both the North American and the Fur Rendezvous dog races.

CHAPTER 30

EMEMBER I SAID WE HAD an eye on the world in that first house? We could watch who went into Terry's Store and who came out. One Saturday, I was talking on the phone and looking out the window when I saw an old man come out of the store. As he walked, suddenly his pants fell down around his ankles. The temperature was, as usual, very cold, and there stood this old man in the middle of the road with no pants and not a stitch of underwear.

In one hand, he held his grocery sack and was frantically trying to pull his pants up with the other hand, but it wasn't working very well. He'd just get one side pulled up, but when he switched the sack to the opposite hand to pull up the other side, the pulled-up side fell down again. He struggled for about five minutes in the subzero cold, and by that time, Mary Starr, who ran Terry's, rushed out the door to the man's aid. She pulled his pants up for him and sent him on his way. There were always out-of-the-ordinary things like that happening in the village.

The one thing that we never lacked in Tanana was a steady supply of characters, and somehow, at one time or another, they all seemed to find their way to our house. Now one of my favorite things to do at that time was make homemade pizza from scratch. One Saturday night, pizza was on the menu for supper, and I remember it was during the North American Dogsled Race, which was held in Fairbanks and was always televised. The village watched collectively since there were always mushers from Tanana competing. On this particular day, a man from the village came over in the afternoon to watch the race with us.

He was carrying a little brown paper sack with a bottle in it, and he said to Jerry, "Do you mind if I have a drink?"

Jerry replied, "Well, it's up to my wife."

Feeling trapped, I just nodded and rolled my eyes. So we sat there in the living room, and every now and then, he took a little nip. The time got later and later, and I wanted to start the pizza, so I told Jerry to ask the man to stay and have supper with us.

I got busy in the kitchen, making the pizza, and when it was finally out of the oven, we sat down at the table to eat. Jerry cut and served the pizza, and we were just beginning to eat when suddenly, without any warning, our guest fell over face first and dead drunk right into his pizza. Cheese and mushrooms went flying, and there he was face down in the pizza.

Now assembling all the necessary ingredients for a homemade pizza in the bush is no small task, to say nothing of the expense, and I guess I would have been mad if it hadn't been so pathetic. So Jerry revived our guest and got him cleaned up, and the man did manage to eat the pizza he'd smashed. Then he got shakily to his feet and asked in slurred speech if he could spend the night.

Jerry said, "No. My wife doesn't want you to stay overnight." He didn't even have to ask me; he just knew. Jerry bundled him up and got him ready to go, and at that point, the man collapsed and fell in the middle of the kitchen and was out cold.

Jerry dripped some water on the man's face and picked him back up and told him he needed to go home. He put him out, and the drunken man was scarcely able to negotiate the steps, but I guess he must have gotten home because we didn't hear of any frozen bodies the next day. That was the last time we invited anybody off the street for pizza.

CHAPTER 31

THE SCHOOL DISTRICT WAS RENTING our house from the Native Corporation, and in November of that first year following the departure of the English teacher and his family, they decided to redo the other side of the building and renovate the apartment. They determined that since our apartment was so big, one of the bedrooms, the one with the bathroom in it, would be part of the new apartment so they wouldn't have to install a whole new bathroom. When it was finished, we ended up with just a three-bedroom place, but we still had more than enough room.

The house was cozy, and I liked living there and wouldn't have minded staying. But we only lived there for one year because the Native Corporation, Tozitna, decided the next year to make the building into their offices. They offered us another place we called the cedar house because it was one of those Lindal Cedar Homes. We looked at the home, and it was a lovely place with a two-car garage, a full basement, a big kitchen, a huge living room, a formal dining room, two bedrooms, and a bath. Upstairs, there were three more bedrooms and another bathroom. It was not furnished and no curtains were provided and the rent was a thousand dollars a month.

I thought the guy was joking when he told me the price, and I just laughed. He suggested we could rent out the upstairs, but we said, "No thanks." It turned out nobody thought it was a good idea no matter how nice the house was because the house sat empty the entire seventeen years I lived in Tanana. If the corporation had asked a more reasonable rent, they could have been making money instead of getting nothing all that time.

So we lived in our house for one year. Jerry left at the first part of May to go down to our boat, which we had left moored in Wrangell. I was to follow when school got out for the summer. In that time, I discovered I had a relative living in the village. R. J. Hayes, my cousin, was working for the Bureau of Land Management and was stationed in Tanana. What a strange coincidence! He had worked for BLM down in his home state of Washington and was transferred to Alaska, and somehow we ended up in the same little town. He arrived in early May, and it was fun to be able to have a relative living so near. But I did enjoy it because it seemed everybody else in town had hundreds of relatives up and down the Yukon, and suddenly I had one too.

RJ was only seasonal during the summer months for about three years, so I really didn't get to see him a lot because he always arrived in May just at the time when we were leaving town for the summer. But at the beginning of fire season and for a short time at the end, I could at least invite him over for dinner.

We spent that first Tanana summer on our boat, and when we came back, we knew that we were going to have to move. It turned out that over the summer, the school had acquired some trailer homes from the old public health service hospital, which had closed down because of disuse. The trailers were already set up, but no one in Tanana had ever lived in them because they had been made ready for occupancy just at the time the hospital closed its doors. They were used trailers and had been barged in from some other public health service facility. But we got one of them, and it was a relief to know that we wouldn't have to move again soon.

We chose one at the far end of the complex, so it was a little bit more private, and it was a big one. There was a living room, a kitchen, three bedrooms (two of them were huge), two bathrooms, and an arctic entry porch. Plus it came with a washer and dryer. We were happy.

When I returned from our summer vacation, Jerry was still down on the boat, so I had to do the moving in. I arrived home after traveling all day, and I was really tired, so I decided to just go to bed and unpack later. I unzipped the suitcase, pulled out my nightgown, and jumped into bed. I fell right asleep, and sometime in the night, I woke up and thought, *What is it I'm touching?*

Something was in the bed, and I couldn't figure out what it was, so I got up and turned on the light. It appeared to be dog food. I thought somebody was playing a trick on me by putting it in my bed because it wasn't even the brand we fed Mitch.

Upon closer inspection, I found mouse tracks all over. The mice were storing the dog food in my bed. I was grossed out! I ripped off my nightgown, threw it in the trash, and jumped into a shower so hot it burned my skin. Then I went back into the bedroom and was scared to death because I just knew the mice were probably curled up in the mattress, just waiting to attack me. I jerked the sheets off the bed and tossed them out on the front porch. Because it was still the middle of the night and because I was not sleeping in that bed again, I moved out to the couch, reluctantly, since I figured there might be mice in there as well.

Luckily, the next day, I was moving into our new trailer. My friend Linda Swenson came over to help with the move, and I told her about my mouse adventure. She laughed and didn't believe it, so I retrieved the sheet and showed her the evidence. She was grossed out too! I pitched the sheets out since I had no intention of ever using them again. When the kids from school came over to help, I made them reach into the cupboards and drawers before I did because I had discovered a mouse nest earlier in one of the dresser drawers. I thought perhaps I was relocating the mice to our new home, but I guess I didn't because we never saw any sign of mice in the new place. Always after that time, we referred to that as the year of the mouse.

So I finally got moved in thanks to all my helpers. The new trailer was filled up with furniture. There were several desks, and it looked like it might have been a depository and storage for all the items nobody knew what else to do with. But eventually, we got settled in and got all the mushrooms cleaned off the floor; they were from the dampness where the window had leaked. It actually cleaned up quite nicely, and we were happy in that house for seven years.

CHAPTER 32

D URING MY NEXT YEAR, I took my class on a cultural awareness field trip to Fairbanks. This was an ambitious enter-
prise and required a lot of preparation. The class wrote and
presented a proposal to the school board, and they in turn granted
us the money. We also approached the Native Council with the same
proposal, and they also donated money for our trip.

What a fantastic time we had, and what wonderful kids they
were to travel with. We explored all kinds of cultural opportunities
not available to us in Tanana. We toured the city fire department, we
went swimming in a real pool, we visited the museum, and we took
a tour of the agricultural farm at the University of Alaska Fairbanks.
As a class, they learned how to ride a city bus, and I took them roll-
er-skating and out for a fancy dinner at a fine restaurant.

Within each experience, there were many learning details for
the students. For instance, in preparation for the dinner, we studied
and discussed table manners and proper restaurant etiquette. We had
chosen a restaurant called Clinkerdagger, Bickerstaff and Petts, an
old English pub type of place in Tudor style. Now we had already
talked about how we should act when we were in public: we wouldn't
run around, and we must sit still patiently and talk quietly while
waiting for our food to be served. Well, the kids were being great little ambassadors, and they were all dressed up in nice clothes. One girl
even wore a beautiful pink hat to match her dress. The boys all had
on suit coats, and they really looked like little ladies and gentlemen.

We were seated in a room by ourselves, and during the course of
the evening, the waitress commented on their good behavior, which
made me very proud to be their teacher. We had the best time, and
they each were allowed to order whatever they wanted, the exception
being that eating hamburgers was not acceptable as a fine dining
experience. I wanted them to choose something they wouldn't nec-

144

essarily be accustomed to eating. I felt they made very good choices and dinner was going along great when one of the boys, Terry Jordan, asked to be excused to go to the bathroom.

I pointed him in the direction of the restrooms, which announced in old English signage, "Lords" and "Ladies". Soon Terry came tearing back, nearly in tears.

"Oh, H," he announced. "There's a bathroom for the ladies and a bathroom for the Lord, but there isn't one for me."

I had a hard time trying not to laugh at his honest mistake, and I explained that because it was an old English tavern, he hadn't understood the signage. Once he understood, he finished his bathroom break.

When the meal was over, we decided to have dessert. The dessert menu offered several choices, and one of them was chocolate mousse. Well, Daphne Huntington was totally perplexed by that. She had eaten moose all her life, and she had never had a chocolate one. I patiently explained what a mousse consisted of and pointed out that even the spellings were different, so she decided to order it. When it arrived, it was actually shaped like a moose, complete with two praline cookies that looked like moose ears, and we all had a good laugh over that.

Earlier in the year, my class had started a school newspaper, so when we got back from our trip, Daphne was assigned to write up an account of the restaurant meal at Clinkerdagger, Bickerstaff and Petts. The whole article turned out to be about chocolate mousse, and it went something like this: "We went to dinner at this fancy restaurant, and what do you think we had? Chocolate mousse! Well, it's not chocolate moose; it's chocolate mousse. But it sounds like *moose* to me. Anyway, when they brought it, it did look like a moose because it had ears on it. But chocolate mousse is not chocolate moose. It's a chocolate pudding, and they put these ears on it with cookies."

To this day, whenever I run into her, even all grown up, Daphne still talks about the chocolate "moose".

That year, the powers that be in Tanana made me, of all people, coordinator of the school spelling bee. I remember calling Mom and telling her about it, and she could not quit laughing and is still laughing over the fact that I was the coordinator of the spelling bee.

Spelling has never been my strong suit; in fact, until I was in junior high school, I thought B-U-R-D was the correct spelling for *bird*. Be that as it may, I was chosen to preside over the event, and I have to say, I really enjoyed it. I didn't have to spell any words, and I had the workbook right in front of me. The kids had to do the actual spelling, and I was relieved that my secret was safe for a while longer.

Around that time, I was also chosen as the coordinator for Battle of the Books, which was a statewide competition where groups of classes in the third, fourth, fifth, and sixth grades were required to read fifteen books and then, over teleconferencing equipment, were required to answer certain questions about those same books. The questions all started with "In which book . . ." The answer always began with the name of a book and the author.

During my second year in Tanana, my team of three fifth graders won the state battle. How exciting that was for me! They were so proud of themselves. There was only one other time we won, but we placed either second, third, or fourth for sixteen years. That's no small accomplishment considering how small our school district was (ninety students total in grades K–12) and the fact that our kids were battling the likes of students from the bigger districts of Fairbanks, Anchorage, and Juneau, where they had a much larger group to pick from. By golly, they did pretty doggoned good, and I was always proud of them.

CHAPTER 33

D URING MY SECOND YEAR IN the village, the class decided they wanted to go on another cultural awareness trip. So I asked, "Where do you want to go this time?" After some consideration, they settled on Anchorage. Now that was a little further than Fairbanks, so I told them we needed to raise some of the money ourselves. That launched a lively discussion of ways we could do that and led to the founding of McTanana.

We made a big sign proclaiming how many burgers we had sold and that we sold not only hamburgers but also french fries and cold pop. I figured making shakes would have been pushing my luck. So we bought all the necessary items—hamburger, buns, large-size jars of mustard, ketchup, and mayonnaise. We added lettuce and frozen french fries to the list, and then I assigned one of the students to write to the McDonald's in Fairbanks and explain what we were doing. That franchise was very accommodating and promptly sent up a supply of paper containers for the fries as well as a big stack of McDonald's napkins, straws, and even hats for the servers to wear. Every Friday night, we set up our makeshift fast-food joint in the gymnasium at the school.

Now there were no restaurants of any kind in Tanana, so people looked forward to McTanana, and business boomed. By the time we finished that year, our sign had been amended to read: "Over 1,000 hamburgers sold." The kids had the best time with that, and they were all very good about pitching in to help. After expenses, they were able to contribute a large sum to the Anchorage fund from McTanana.

We held a lot of fund-raising projects to raise money for the trip to Anchorage, and by golly, we made it. It was again called a cultural awareness trip, but this time, we had earned every penny ourselves.

We went to Anchorage and stayed at the Holiday Inn because it had a swimming pool and that was a big drawing card for the kids. We visited the Imaginarium, which was a museum for kids. We went for a ride on a tugboat, the one Jerry had worked on when we lived in Anchorage. We explored the city zoo, we visited a bank to observe how it operated, we toured McDonald's, we watched the daily operations at the *Anchorage Daily News*, we took a train ride from Anchorage to Whittier, and we ate at another fancy restaurant. One of the things the class wanted to do was try different kinds of foods, so on this trip, I introduced them to Japanese and Thai styles of cooking. Prior to our trip, the students had taken turns writing to each stop on our tour, requesting permission for a visit. Other students were assigned the task of checking into other types of suitable attractions the city might have to offer.

Another adventure the kids learned in Anchorage was how to ride a city bus. Some of them had never had that experience since there were no buses in Tanana. So the kids paired off, and each pair boarded a different bus, each one of which made a loop and then returned downtown. Well, one of the buses broke down in the middle of its route, and all the passengers had to evacuate the bus with no further instructions.

The two students followed everyone else out of the bus but were told they couldn't make any telephone calls because the phone service happened to be out also. Well, the point of their drop-off was a hospital about five miles from where they were expected to be, and they were unfamiliar with their surroundings. This particular situation hadn't been discussed, and they were a little bewildered as to what they should do. After talking about it, they decided the obvious solution was to try to call H, but that was when they discovered there was no phone service, so that plan wasn't going to work.

Cheryl Folger, one of the student pair, suggested they could find a cab and return to the hotel, and that was just what they did. When they arrived back at the hotel, they came to my room and found me so I could pay the cab fare. I was so proud of them, and as soon as she saw me, Cheryl started crying. I said, "Honey, don't cry now. You did exactly the right thing, and you made a good choice.

You knew you needed to get back, and you figured out what to do. You did well!"

The class was intrigued by and loved everything about that trip. Their favorite part was when we all got back to the hotel and they got to swim in the pool. Again, it was enjoyable to go with them, and we all had a wonderful time.

One year when we didn't have much money to work with, we only traveled as far as Manley Hot Springs. It was close, and my class that year had expressed an interest in learning how to swim. So when they found out the hotel in Manley had a pool, it was unanimous we should go there. That was another successful trip and a lot of fun.

We stayed at the hotel for three days and the school at Manley invited us to come down and visit and we all enjoyed that. We also visited a hydroponic garden grown by a lady who also had an enclosed garden over a hot spring so she could garden all year long. She even grew grapes, and the kids were really interested in that since they had never seen the way grapes grew.

Now, getting to Manley was an adventure in itself. You had to take a smaller airplane than the one that flew from Fairbanks to Tanana because the Manley runway was very short. So we flew into the village in shifts since the plane only seated six, but we finally all arrived and got settled in the lodge.

One year, the lodge offered us the use of their van, and we all drove down to the dump. I know that sounds crazy, but it was the most beautiful dump I've ever seen. It sat high on a hill overlooking the Yukon River and not only did it offer a spectacular view of the surrounding area but it was also a very clean dump. Unlike other landfills, people were required to dig holes and bury their garbage rather than just throw it in helter-skelter.

From the dump, we drove down to the Tanana River to the boat landing and walked to the one and only store in town to buy junk food, and on the way, we visited Joe Reddington's dog yard. Joe was a famous Alaskan Iditarod racer and had his kennels in Manley. He was nice enough to show us his award-winning dogs and some of his sleds.

Now, the main purpose of this particular trip was that the kids all wanted to learn to swim, so mainly that was what we did. We ate and swam and swam and ate. At night, everyone looked like very wrinkled prunes, but by the time the trip was over, each one of them knew how to swim and swam very well. I was proud of them.

CHAPTER 34

I REMEMBER ONE WINTER DURING THE seven years we lived in that first trailer when we had so much snow the house was almost completely covered with it. Only the tops of the windows peeked out from the white mounds. It was amazing.

A couple of times, the electricity went out in the winter for extended periods. But we were able to hang a blanket up at the door of the hallway and close the bedroom door in the front, so that only left the kitchen and living room to be heated. We opened up our stove, which ran on propane, and heated the house that way. Once, when the temperature got to fifty below, the power went out, and school was dismissed, so there was no place to go to keep warm. We had to flush the toilet every ten or fifteen minutes so it wouldn't freeze. We made it through okay, but even I must admit that it was a little bit chilly.

Apart from that time, school never closed. Even on the year the temperature dropped to seventy-six below zero, the school never closed. I don't know if you've ever experienced seventy-six degrees below zero, but I can tell you, it is *cold*. It was so cold it's just beyond belief and defies description. It was so cold you could actually feel ice on your eyeballs.

At that time, we only lived about a hundred yards from the school, and I still had to dress in everything I owned just to get to school. But the school stayed open because it was the only warm place for the kids to go. Parents were going crazy because most of the families lived in very small houses. Winter days were dark and seemed to go on forever, and tempers ran short. So the school stayed open, but nobody ventured outdoors if they didn't have to, although I did conduct an outdoor science experiment with my class.

We boiled some water and took it in cups to just outside the door of the school and threw it up in the air as far as we could. We wanted to see if it would come down, and I can now tell you, it does not! I guarantee that because we proved it. The water just sort of "poofed" and left a big cloud like dry ice, but it didn't come down. Then we tried throwing water at each other, but before it made contact, it had evaporated. That was an interesting experiment that, I'm sure, not many teachers get to try in their lifetime.

The temperature stayed at sixty below or more for about a month, and when it got up to fifty below, we thought we were having a heat wave. Then when it got to twenty below, people were running around with no coats on. Where you live makes a big difference in what you think is cold and what isn't.

One January day in the winter of 1986, when the temperature registered somewhere about forty below, the plane came in. It was a Mark Air, and they had bigger planes that were able to fly in weather that cold. I was supposed to be going to Fairbanks to do a reading in-service for the Yukon-Koyukuk school district, so I decided to fly in since the plane was there.

Well, it was so cold Jerry couldn't even get the snow machine running to take me to the airport. The shuttles weren't running for the same reason, so we called for the taxi, which managed to make it through the cold weather and took me out to the airport. So I boarded the plane, and believe me when I tell you, it was as cold inside the cabin as it was outside.

By the time I got into Fairbanks and got off the plane, besides being half frozen, I realized I didn't have my purse with me. I had left it home! The nice lady who met the plane asked if I was Suzanne Henning. When I nodded, she told me, "Your husband called and said you have no money, but everything is taken care of."

I was pretty happy to hear that. I picked up my suitcase and hailed a cab.

The lady at the airport had said not to worry about the cab fare because Jerry had called the Yukon-Koyukuk School District and someone was to meet me at the hotel when I arrived to pay the driver. So I climbed in the cab, and the visibility was near zero because of the ice fog. I didn't know how that driver could see anything, but I realized that, after living here in Fairbanks, he knew where he was even if I didn't.

Well, we were traveling down Airport Road, and there was a chain link fence bordering it, but of course, I couldn't see that. I could not see the street signs hanging overhead at each crossroad until we were right underneath them. I couldn't even make out the traffic lights as we crept along, and the ice fog just seemed to get worse.

Eventually, the driver pulled up to the hotel, and a representative of Yukon-Koyukuk came out and paid the fare and helped me in with my bags. She said Jerry had arranged for me to go to the bank and get some money since, along with my money, my purse contained my identification, the checkbook, my comb, and all those necessary little items all women would have stashed in their purses.

Luckily for me, given the dense ice fog and the temperature reading of 50 below zero, the bank we did business with was located directly across the street from the hotel. I think God must have intervened somewhere along the line because I can't even think now of another hotel with a bank right across the street from it. I bundled myself up again and plodded across the street to the bank.

Except for a couple of employees, the place was empty, so I walked up to one of the service windows, ready to explain my predicament.

I said to the teller, "I've got a problem."

She looked at me quite calmly and said, "You're Suzanne Henning." It was a statement, not a question. "Your husband called, so we've been expecting you. And besides, who else would be out in this weather but somebody who didn't have any money?"

We had a good laugh, and I was able to get some money, but I still had no credentials. I remember I had to give my mother's maiden name as identification to get the money, but I did get it.

About two blocks from the bank was a grocery store, so I hiked down there and bought some necessary grooming items, and I was back in business.

I completed the in-service, and the next day, I was to fly back home. Mark Air was still flying. It was forty-five below, and that was their cutoff point, past which they would not take off. Forty below was the cutoff for the smaller airlines, like Warbelow's, Larry's Air, and Frontier. So I got on that plane, and it turned out to be the last plane that flew into Tanana for the next fifteen days because the temperature plunged to seventy-six below zero, and nothing flew then. So I was really lucky to be back home.

CHAPTER 35

O N THE DAY IT GOT to seventy-six below zero, we did have school. That was the only warm place in town. Parents wanted their kids to be in school to get them out of their hair, and the kids wanted to be there too because most of the homes had only outhouses and the school had indoor plumbing. The next day, it was decided that the school would close even though it was only sixty-six below zero that day. But the parents objected, so sometime in the afternoon, we reopened the school so the kids would have someplace to go. But the bus wasn't running because it was too cold, so the students either had to walk to the school, or parents had to bring them in on snow machines. There wasn't ever a lot of absenteeism because school in the bush was a diversion for kids and they wanted to be there.

On those really cold days, I had to wear almost every piece of clothing I owned just to get to school. It took me at least ten or fifteen minutes to get dressed in my outside gear. I wore long johns and snow pants, a turtleneck T-shirt, a sweater, a coat, a scarf, mitts, and goggles. You must cover every part of your body because, at those temperatures, it's instant burn and frostbite.

The temperature stayed at fifty below or more for about four or five weeks, and it was miserable. Some people's heating oil jelled up like Vaseline. Ours didn't, thank heavens, but we lived in a trailer at the time, and what we did notice was that we could tell how cold it was by how far the frost had crept up the walls inside our house. At the coldest point, the ice on our walls was about four feet high. It was amazing to watch.

Our furnace ran nonstop, and we, of course, didn't have a wood-burning stove. We didn't sleep much at night because our ears were attuned to the furnace to make sure it was still running. We did make it through that time okay. We had plenty of food. We didn't always have what we wanted, but we didn't starve either. The store shelves were totally wiped out. There was no bread, milk, or any of the necessities, and after about two weeks, even the fancy stuff that nobody ever bought, which had been on the shelves for years, had been snapped up.

Besides learning to like food you wouldn't eat normally, another thing you'd find out in times of crisis like that was that you'd better like the people you lived with a lot because you'd be stuck inside together all the time. But we had lots of things that filled our time. We played cribbage, and Jerry liked to read, so he did a lot of that. He had his workshop, and I had my sewing room, so we kept ourselves busy. We tried not to go outside the house for any reason whatsoever, and if we did, it was only for ten minutes at a time.

That was the coldest winter I've ever experienced in my life, and I hope never to experience another like it. Even Mitch knew better than to go outside for any length of time. My boss's wife had made the dog designer booties for Christmas, the kind designed for sled dogs. Mitch made it plain from the beginning he was not a sled dog and wouldn't have anything to do with them—until the temperature dropped to seventy-six below, and then he consented to let us put them on his feet. But as soon as his business was completed and he was back inside, he let us know he wanted them off—now! He was a shorthaired dog so his coat wasn't much protection from the cold, and I think he felt it down to his bones.

We learned from experience that we couldn't mop the floors when it was that cold either, especially in a trailer. With its minimal insulation, the floor didn't dry; it froze, and we had our very own skating rink.

We did what we could to keep our place warm, like banking the trailer by taking the snow and piling it up around the edge of the house to keep the heat underneath. I think that did help some, but at seventy-six below, nothing helped much. We had to keep a trickle of water running all the time so the pipes wouldn't freeze. Our kitchen was in the center of the house, and there was a bathroom on each end, so with the bathroom sinks running, the kitchen faucet was fine.

Now if an emergency arose in the bush and someone should need medical help that couldn't be provided by the physician's assistant at the health center, the patient had to be flown into Fairbanks for treatment. In the extremely cold weather, though, the planes couldn't fly, so the physician's assistant was on edge all the time since she was on her own. We all just prayed and hoped nothing would come up she couldn't handle.

I remember when it finally warmed up that year and the first plane came in; the whole town was thrilled. We hadn't had newspapers, fresh milk, vegetables, or fruit in a long time, so it was really pretty exciting. And once the planes started coming in, they came in a steady stream, so we were able to get back to normal.

CHAPTER 36

D URING MY SECOND YEAR IN Tanana, the school board decided not to renew Bob Jackman's contract, so we got a new superintendent, Ken Lease. Ken was there for about three years, and somewhere in the middle of his second term, he asked me if I wanted to go to the math consortium of which our school district was a member. He explained two people were needed from each member district to attend the meeting. At first, I said no, and then I decided to open myself up to new horizons, so I agreed to attend.

It was in the summer of 1986 that I first attended the Alaska Math Consortium, and from then on, I was hooked. I absolutely loved being a part of most of it. The classes were held at the University of Alaska Fairbanks, and it was a four-week course. The downside was that everyone was housed in the dormitories. Believe it or not, that was my first experience in dorm living and, hopefully, my last.

It was a coed dorm, which I really didn't like. First of all, I didn't like having to share a bathroom with other women, much less having to share it with men. Then, my room was like a cell. The bed and desk were bolted to the wall and couldn't be moved. It was very hot that summer, and of course, there was no air-conditioning, so I rented a fan for my little cubicle of a room. As you can probably guess, that wasn't much help, but it did stir the air around.

When I got up in the middle of the night to use the bathroom, I wandered down the hall in my nightgown and bathrobe and prayed I wouldn't meet some man with the same idea. I think maybe when I was eighteen, dorm living might have been cool, but a woman over forty looks at the situation from a totally different perspective. It just wasn't my idea of fun.

Other than the living conditions, I really enjoyed that math consortium, and it was through that I became much more competent in teaching math. And through that organization, I started presenting a lot more math in-services, traveling to places such as Kotzebue, Healy, Fairbanks, and several other locations down on the Kenai Peninsula.

During my third year in Tanana, instead of teaching fourth and fifth grades, I was moved to the sixth and seventh grades. So now, although I was in my third year of teaching in the village, I still had the same group of students I'd started with. I loved every one of them, and they will go down in history as my favorite group of kids.

Well, that year, the kids decided they wanted to go on yet another trip, and this time, they selected Juneau. That was fine with me. We seemed to be working our way around Alaska and learning as we went, so we started raising money once again. We held raffles, we made quilts, and the kids planned and executed a fund-raising Christmas bazaar for the rest of the school and the teachers.

One of the items we made for the bazaar was a little book the students compiled themselves entitled *How Many Things Are in Tanana, Alaska?* They counted everything they could think of to count in town. They counted the number of airplanes (12), computers (20 privately owned and 51 in the school), people (363); women over 18 (101), children under 18 (130), men over 18 (132), dogs (534), cars (23), trucks (67), etc. Then we put all the information together and made it up into a little 22-page booklet, which we sold at the bazaar for one dollar each.

We also decided to make up a birthday calendar by collecting the birth dates of all the people in town, and we wrote the names on a calendar we designed and sold those for two dollars. The calendars were a big hit and became an annual fund-raiser for my classroom.

Although we began by selling just a few items the class had made, in the second year, we offered a little more variety. By the third year, we held a bazaar, and we were busy from the start of the school year until Christmas, making items to sell.

We opened the bazaar up to the community and rented out tables for ten dollars each to townspeople with various craft items to sell. We called it the Christmas Marketplace, and it was an instant success. The response from the community was marvelous.

Everybody came. It was definitely the place to be and be seen. There were different organizations within the school that wanted tables to offer their wares; the education association even took several tables and held a used-book sale. It was a great way for the community to come together.

There were lots of crafters in town; for example, one of the men made clocks out of burls, and he displayed and sold those. We had people selling pickled salmon bellies and smoked fish. The Catholic church sponsored a table with all sorts of handmade scarves and beadwork and lots of other beautifully crafted things. We had tables with homemade jewelry, and even the basketball team took a space and sold ice-cream sundaes. The imagination of the village was endless, and our little bazaar grew and became one of the high points of the year.

Our birthday calendars were a big hit because they did include the whole village and everybody liked to see their name in print. We made about one hundred calendars and sold them for two dollars apiece. The production costs were almost nothing because the school did the printing on their copier. The kids did all the work of collating and stapling, and the card stock we used had been included in my yearly classroom order. The money we made from the sale of them was pure profit, so they knew they were guaranteed at least two hundred dollars. The class also sold a few original handmade Christmas tree ornaments—folded paper stars, yarn octopuses, angels from tin can lids, and bells.

Another item we offered were some clever little book bags we designed ourselves. The Catholic church had donated a bunch of old blue jeans. We cut them apart and cut off the legs so that the book bag itself was the "body" of the pants, complete with zippers and pockets. Then we cut a strap from the discarded legs and attached it to the bag so it could be worn over the shoulder. The bags turned out really cute and were good sellers. Altogether, my class netted almost five hundred dollars toward their Juneau trip, and they were tickled pink.

Each month leading up to the trip, we planned something else to raise money. One month, we had a school-wide rummage sale in our classroom in addition to our McTanana nights, so by spring, our trip was completely financed and paid for. They were pretty proud of themselves and rightly so. Again they had done all the research and written for the information and made all the reservations. The planning and execution of our trips were a total learning experience for the whole class.

In early May, we flew to Fairbanks and then on to Juneau, the state capital, where we stayed for four days. There was just one other teacher, a man, and myself for chaperones. While I slept in the same room as the girls, the other teacher refused to sleep in the same room with the boys, so he had the room next door to theirs. During the sightseeing part of our tour, it was just the class and me. Fortunately, my classes never numbered more than ten.

We visited the senate building where we were introduced to all the state senators. We toured the governor's mansion and visited the governor himself, and he gave the kids their own personal seminar on the basics of state government. Many of the students had never been to the ocean, so we made a point of going there and even checked out a glacier. We also paid a visit to the Alaska State Museum.

When we arrived in Juneau, we rented cars, and that turned out to be a big hit with all the kids. They loved just riding around the streets of the city because they liked to look at the green grass. In Tanana, grass, when there was any, was dried and brown, so seeing all the lush green lawns was quite exciting for them.

From Juneau, we boarded the ferry for Sitka, which stopped in several small towns along the way. When we docked in Angoon, we got off the ferry to visit with the auntie of George Woods, one of the boys in my class. She came down to the boat, so everyone got to meet her, and then we reboarded the ferry and went on to Sitka.

Again we rented cars and stayed at a big hotel with a pool, and we had a blast. Here we visited Sheldon Jackson College and had breakfast with James Michener, the author, who was spending some time there to do research for his novel, *Alaska*. The kids were thrilled to meet an authentic author. Also, while at the college, the class had an opportunity to watch native crafts being made, and they learned about the native people of the southeast called Tlingits.

We all paid a visit to my former Sitka neighbors, Coke and Gary Oines, who had invited us for a cookout. The kids thought it was great having hotdogs and s'mores around a fire.

At the end of the week, we caught the ferry back to Juneau and flew home from there. The kids had had another enlightening trip and a grand time. They were all so well behaved it was just a joy to travel with them.

CHAPTER 37

THE BIRTHDAY CALENDAR FUND-RAISER WAS such a success that it also became an annual class project. Eventually, we raised the price to three dollars, and we were producing about two hundred calendars per year and making money hand over fist, so we decided to incorporate. The class had ownership of the company, one student was responsible for contacting the government patent office, and we were given a small emblem, which showed a smiley face surrounded by the words "Tanana Calendar Company" and the date of incorporation underneath it.

Each calendar was collated and stapled to a backing, and near the top on the backing, the students drew elaborate illustrations. The pictures were absolutely gorgeous, and the people liked them so well they requested the kids sign them, so they did.

Each year on the day before Thanksgiving, we made our room into a factory. I always accompanied that with a lesson about working in factories with an emphasis on assembly lines because that was the way we assembled the calendars. The kids were divided by jobs—staplers, collators, hole punchers, and artists. I appointed a floor boss, whose job it was to check proper placement of the staples, keep the staplers filled, sharpen pencils, and act as an overseer to make sure each student was doing his job. Stations were set up all around the room like an assembly line, and every fifteen minutes, they changed jobs and earned a two-minute break.

The first calendar off the assembly line each year was presented to our school superintendent, so each year, he made a special appearance to receive his calendar and to have his picture taken with whoever the floor boss was at that moment, making the presentation. I couldn't believe how popular those birthday calendars became and how the whole thing just mushroomed. It was amazing.

Another interesting project we started about the same time as the bazaar was the celebration of Tanana Week, which was the brainchild of one of the teachers, Van Mitchell. It was a chance for all the classes and teachers to explore the outdoors and learn about the things we had in our area. We did a lot of things that involved the Yukon River and took advantage of what the land offered us.

For instance, one year we picked blueberries and had a lesson in making a blueberry pie. We dissected fish as a biology experiment. We checked out the speed of the river by having a junk race. That involved the kids finding pieces of trash and then making something out of it that would float, and then we used a stopwatch and held timed races. The races then became a series of math problems (i.e., the average time of all the race entries, how many minutes the races took altogether, which was the fastest, which was the slowest, and what was the difference between them). It was really a fun thing to do, and my classes really got into it.

I remember the year my sister visited during Tanana Week. The classes traveled by school bus to the White Alice site and picked weeds to see who could find the tallest weed, and we measured it in inches and then converted it to centimeters. One year we even learned how to make a campfire without using any paper.

On the last day of Tanana Week, we usually went on an outing, weather permitting. We packed our backpacks with food and trudged off to the woods. We built fires and cooked and made tea over the campfire, and I always sent the kids on a nature scavenger hunt to find various things.

Once, we performed a biosphere experiment where I gave the kids a piece of string, and they had to make a circle out of it and lay it down on the ground and see what they could get out of that one small circle of land, like a bug or a plant or something that was in that specific sphere.

One year, we held a contest. I divided the kids into groups and gave each group a packet containing matches, a piece of newspaper, teabags, cups, a big coffee can, and water. They had to build a fire and boil the water and make tea. The group that finished first was declared the winner, and I always had some kind of prize for the winners of each event. They had the best time and learned a lot while they were enjoying themselves. No matter where we chose to go for our experiments, if they were held outside of town, we always had to have somebody along with a gun because there was the constant danger of bears.

Bears were especially numerous at the White Alice site, which was seven miles out of town, up a steep hill. Sometimes we chose the lake out past the dump. Some years, when the weather was too bad, we just stayed around the school and did our lessons, but it was always an enjoyable week for me and for the students.

I don't think I ever had a student that I disliked the entire time I taught in that village. I had some I didn't like as well as others, but I really made an effort to treat each of them equally. That said, in any teaching career, there are always a few students that will always stand out in memory.

CHAPTER 38

As I said before, during my first year in Tanana, I had a great bunch of students, but Stephanie Swenson sticks out in my mind. That girl was something. She was the daughter of one of our teachers, Linda Swenson. Linda was actually the reason I was teaching fifth grade that first year. Linda had been teaching that class, but she didn't want to have her daughter in her class, so I was assigned a split class of fourth and fifth grades. Well, Stephanie was just a doll, and I absolutely loved her. She reminded me so much of my niece Janie, which might have been part of the reason I liked her so well.

Several times, when Linda had to be out of town for teachers' meetings, Stephanie stayed at our house overnight. I remember, on one occasion around Christmastime when she stayed, I had bought some latch hook rugs for the class to do for our bazaar. So the two of us worked on those late into the evening, and the next morning, as we were walking to school, she said, "Wow, H, this is really cool—two hookers walking to school."

Of course, she didn't realize the implication of her remark, but I thought it was kind of funny, and so did her mother when I related the incident to her.

The other thing about Stephanie was, she always had "owies." She was always hurt, and she always wrapped the hurts with an Ace bandage, so we nicknamed her Ace. Just a bump from a minor fall was reason enough for an Ace bandage as far as she was concerned.

I remember one time the school received a bunch of shoe-type roller skates, and we were given permission to roller-skate in the gym. Some of the students had no idea how to roller-skate, so I was going to teach them. We were making pretty good progress when Stephanie fell down. She rolled around on the gym floor as if she was in horrible pain, and I really thought she had injured herself. I hurried down to Linda's classroom to report the accident. The next day, Stephanie showed up in class like nothing had happened. Linda explained to me later that Stephanie had recovered miraculously by wrapping an Ace bandage around her bottom. As I said, it seemed to be the cure-all for everything. That Christmas, I gave her a whole box of Ace bandages, and she was thrilled. They lasted for a long time.

Stephanie nicknamed me the High Mucky-Muck, and she gave me a mug that year for Christmas with that inscription on it. But she shortened the name to Mucky-Muck, so it would fit on the cup.

One year at Christmastime, I gave the kids a writing assignment for a how-to essay. The subject choice was theirs, but they had to put all the directions in writing. It was a classroom assignment, so when they had finished and handed them in, we went on to do some silent reading. The room was very quiet as I began to read over and correct the writing papers. Stephanie's paper was on the top, and when I read it, I started laughing out loud. I couldn't control myself. She had very explicitly described how to decorate a Christmas tree as follows: "First, you go out and cut the tree down, and then you put the lights on it. Then you put the icicles on." She very systematically listed each step, and she ended by saying, "The last thing you do is hang Santa's balls." We had been studying apostrophes, and she had correctly used the rule, but it came out unexpectedly peculiar.

I excused myself and went down to show it to her mom, and we both had a good laugh. I kept that paper for a long time, and later, when Stephanie was in her midtwenties, I gave it back to her. She said she remembered that day when I had laughed so hard, but she couldn't figure out what was so funny.

One of my favorite class projects was a school newspaper, and the kids had a lot of fun with that. It began as *The Elementary News* but was later renamed to *Wolf Tracks* because the school's sports teams were called the Wolves. We included all kinds of school-related articles in our paper, and the kids learned some valuable English grammar lessons.

Each month, a different student was chosen to act as editor in chief, and the kids did all the typing and the printing and collating and then sold the papers for a quarter apiece. These proceeds also went into our trip fund. The class had fun with this project, and the stories were quite unique. Right from the beginning, I kept the originals of all those stories, and when my students started graduating from high school, I presented them with the old copies of the newspaper stories they had written.

That turned out to be a real hit with my former students, and kids complained if, for their graduation present, they didn't get an old newspaper with their articles in it or a copy from the month they had acted as editor. That was always fun, and it was also fun for the students to go back and look at those newspapers and see how much their writing had improved.

That first class included Ginger Kennedy, but by the time she was in high school, her family had moved to Beaver, Alaska. There was no high school in Beaver, so Ginger was sent to Mount Edgecumbe in Sitka, which was a state-owned high school operated by the Bureau of Indian Affairs. She wrote me a letter, thanking me for teaching her how to write articles for a newspaper because that was something she had to do in high school. I treasure her letter to this day. I think it's neat that a young person would think back, at high school level, to a time in fourth grade when they first learned how to do something. It made me feel very good.

One of my other favorite students of all time was Nathan Mitchell. What a joy it was to have him in my class. He was the son of one of our teachers, Van Mitchell. Van and Nathan moved to Tanana around 1985, and at the time they arrived, Nathan was in the third grade and was having a miserable time in that room because the teacher didn't seem to like him and singled him out repeatedly for scoldings. Van fought hard to have Nathan transferred to my classroom. At the time, I was teaching a combined class of fourth, fifth, and sixth graders, and Nathan was a welcome addition to my classroom. He was a smart boy and could do some of the fourth-grade-level work. I taught him for three years, and he was like a breath of fresh air, always coming up with new and innovative ideas.

Van was a single parent at that time, and besides being a teacher, he was also the basketball and ski coach. When he had to go out of town with the teams or for any other reason, Nathan would stay with Jerry and me. He was one of the nicest kids to have stayed with us, and to this day, I still keep in touch with him. He became a Navy SEAL, and when he graduated from the Navy SEAL's academy, he sent me an invitation to the ceremony. It was at Christmastime, and I couldn't attend because it was on the last day of school before Christmas vacation and the school policy wouldn't allow me to have that day off.

It was while Van was teaching in Tanana that he met his future wife, Kama, who was a teacher in Anchorage. Jerry and I were invited to the wedding, and after that, Kama moved out to Tanana for a year. The two of us became good friends. Even after that, Nathan still enjoyed visiting at our house for overnights.

The last word I had is that when he is discharged from the navy, he intends to go back to school to become an elementary teacher "just like H." I am touched by the fact that I made a difference in a child's life. When you're a teacher, sometimes there are days when you think you are not really reaching anybody or that you aren't doing what you need to do. So when you hear about the joys and successes of former students, it just brings tears to your eyes to know that you have touched a life in one way or another. Sometimes teachers never know whose lives they may have touched or how unless they're told, and it is truly heartwarming and rewarding.

Another of my other favorite students at that time was Angela Drennan. Angie was a sweetheart. Her father worked for the Federal Aviation Administration, and he was transferred to Tanana for a year. She was in fourth grade, and she was a beautiful child and a joy to have in class. It was also pleasant to work with her parents because they were so involved in her schoolwork. I became good friends with that family and still keep in touch with them.

Sixteen years later, Angie was married in Colorado, and I attended her wedding. What an honor to be remembered after all those years.

There are just so many kids who were my favorites I can't remember them all: Julia Sweetsir, Amber Bowen, Willow Bowen, Terry Jordan—and oh yes, Terry Jordan. He was in my first Tanana class, and he was a challenge, but I absolutely loved him. He lived with his grandmother, and together they shared a life of subsistence, so his diet consisted mainly of dried fish, smoked fish, and moose meat. Well, let me tell you, that kind of diet gave him horrible gas problems. I never knew such a little kid could have such big gas attacks.

I finally took him aside and told him that kind of behavior was not acceptable in public and we just couldn't pass gas whenever and wherever we felt like it. Actually, none of the kids in the villages understood that concept well. To them, it was a fact of life. So I tried to teach them using all the polite euphemisms, and finally, I told Terry, "Now look! If you feel you have to pass gas, get up and excuse yourself and go out in the hallway. It isn't funny." Well, that just cracked him up, but I apparently got my point across. It took a while, but I finally got them trained.

Terry Jordan enlisted in the army and was sent to Haiti. While he was in the service, I received a letter from him every two weeks, and I loved it. Terry's handwriting was awful; in fact, he was the first student I ever taught to type just so he could use the computer because I simply couldn't read his writing. But he faithfully wrote to me, and I painstakingly deciphered the letters. He described his life and work in Haiti, and it was such a treat to receive those letters. Terry's mother, Lorraine, was the postmistress in Tanana, so she always knew when I got a letter from Terry and waited anxiously for news of her son.

When he was discharged from military service, he returned to Tanana and was hired as a substitute teacher at the school. Every time he subbed, he would come into my classroom and tell my students what a wonderful teacher they had and that they had better listen to me because I really cared about them.

That really touched me. Here was a man who'd seen horrible things happen in Haiti because he had served during a time of particular unrest in that country. And for him to come back and give me such credit meant a lot to me.

There were a couple more things about Terry's elementary school experience. Every once in a while, I'd make the kids clean out their desks. Now the lid of Terry's desk would never completely close because he had so much stuff in it. Well, that one particular day I'm thinking of, when he cleaned out the contents of his desk, he found four pairs of socks and a shirt. Then we also checked the lost-and-found department, where Terry reclaimed thirteen shirts, three sweaters, and two towels. I don't know what he had left in his closet at home, but I'm sure his grandma thought he had a whole new wardrobe when he came home from school that day.

I regularly gave an award to the person with the messiest desk, and it was consistently Terry who received the infamous Pigpen award, although there were times when that dubious honor had to be mine. The kids had come up with the design of the award themselves. It was a cross-stitch pattern with the inscription "Pigpen Sweet Pigpen." The winner had the honor of keeping the award until the next time we cleaned out our desks.

In addition to his many virtues, if you could call them that, Terry was a junk-food junkie. By the time he got to sixth grade, he could consume three candy bars in three bites and was very proud of that talent. In one of his letters I received from Haiti, he complained of suffering because he couldn't get his favorite junk food down there.

CHAPTER 39

THE YEAR 1985 WAS ALSO the year I had my "nose job." I had been having breathing problems for some time, and Jerry thought I should see a doctor, so I could "get it fixed" as he put it. So I went into Fairbanks for an appointment with Dr. Raugust, an ear, nose, and throat specialist. He agreed I did have some problems.

"Your sinuses are infected, and they need to be scraped, but I need to hear what you sound like, so I want you to make a tape recording of yourself snoring," he told me.

So we went back home, and Jerry said he would make the tape. The next morning, there was a horrible sound coming from the tape recorder. It was my snoring, and it was so bad I couldn't believe it. Tears came to my eyes. It sounded like a sick cow: "Mmmmmmmooooooooooooo." It just went on and on, and I knew then why Jerry complained of not being able to sleep himself. So I took that evidence to Dr. Raugust and told him my name was on the tape. "But if I ever find that anyone else knows about this, I'll have to kill you."

He listened to it and immediately diagnosed it as sleep apnea. I would snore like a sailor for a while and then stop breathing and then resume snoring. The doctor gave me three options: (1) scrape my sinuses, (2) fix the deviated septum in my nose (which he suspected had been broken at birth and not noticed), and (3) if neither of those worked, he could remove my uvula. I told him to do all three and get it over with.

So all three procedures were scheduled, and I made a date with the hospital. I was told that doing all three at one time was highly unusual, and I do remember there were several doctors in the operating room to observe my operations.

I remember when I came out of the anesthetic that I was screaming for Jerry. The next thing I remember is hearing the *ding, ding, ding* of the elevator as they returned me to the surgical floor. As they pushed the gurney down the hallway, I remember looking up at a sign that identified the service on that floor, and that was what I focused on—the sign that read Psychiatric Ward.

Now Dr. Raugust had warned me that, following my surgery, I couldn't cry because my nose was going to be packed. So if I cried, there wouldn't be any way for the mucus to come out. Well, I really wanted to cry because my first thought was that I had been so unmanageable during my surgery they had to put me on the mental floor. As it turned out, the floor I was going to was located right next door to the psych ward, but I wasn't in the psych ward.

I stayed in the hospital for two nights, and the reason they kept me even one night was because I lived in the bush. I had had three separate procedures done, so the doctors wanted to be sure I was going to be all right before they sent me home. That was just a horrible time. I had a hard time swallowing because they had removed my uvula, and I couldn't breathe through my nose because of all the packing. I was a mess! It was an ordeal to even take a sip of water. I had to drink it from a spoon because I couldn't suck through a straw. I was hungry, but I couldn't eat anything because I couldn't swallow.

Finally, after two days, they did let me out, but we had to stay in town four more days because I had to go back to the doctor to have the packing removed from my nose. Doctor Raugust assured me my throat would heal. Of course, the incision had stitches, and one of the threads was hanging down, so it always felt like there was something in my throat. I was always trying to swallow, but it wouldn't go away.

The doctor told me I could eat soft things, and by this time, I was kind of hungry because all I'd had to eat was some water and juice and Jell-O, and even that was hard to swallow. But I needed something to eat, so I told Jerry some mashed potatoes and gravy really sounded good; that would be soft. So we found a restaurant, and I ordered mashed potatoes and gravy. And what do you think? I was served hamburger gravy, and it had lumps in it, so I still couldn't eat it. I was really disappointed because I had been expecting plain gravy with no lumps, so I was still hungry.

I did manage to survive, and before we flew home, the doctor gave me some liquid morphine. I don't know what was worse—the pain or swallowing that horrible medicine. Because I was still having trouble swallowing, I had to hold the liquid in my mouth and get it situated just right so I could swallow it. It was really bad-tasting stuff, and I hope I never have to take it again.

I was out of school for three weeks that time, but I did heal up nicely. I still snore but not nearly as bad as I did before the operation. And as an added bonus, it was the first time in my entire life I remember being able to breathe out of both sides of my nose at once. And I could really smell things. All those years, I didn't realize that you could breathe through both nostrils, and smells became so much more clear and pungent. Also, before the operation, I had sinus infections all the time, but since then, I only had a couple. So scraping my sinuses, taking out my uvula, and repairing my deviated septum, while it might have been unusual, really worked, and I'm glad I chose to have it done all at once.

CHAPTER 40

BLUEBERRY PICKING IN TANANA WAS one of my favorite things to do, and Jerry and I had our favorite spot up past the White Alice site where the old airstrip had been located. Every fall, we would get on our three-wheelers and go up to pick berries. We'd always make a day of it and take our lunch. It was about seven miles up to the site and then about two miles back into where we actually picked. Usually, we would go with other people. It was so much fun, but Jerry always took his gun since the danger of bears was ever present.

I remember one time after Jerry died when I went up picking with my boss and his wife and Sandy Mangold, my next-door neighbor. We picked for quite a while and were on our way back out with Sandy and I in the lead when we came upon the biggest bear print I had ever seen in my life. I knew it hadn't been there when we went in. It scared Sandy so bad she dropped her berry pail, which was full to the brim, and she didn't even stop to pick them up.

Berry picking was always a great time, and we always got enough so that we could freeze them and have blueberry muffins and blueberry pancakes for the entire winter. I miss the berry picking here in Fairbanks. If you want to pick blueberries here, you have to go a long way out of town, and you can never be guaranteed there will be berries. So now I go to Safeway to buy my winter supply of blueberries. It's not nearly as much fun, but I figure six bucks for enough berries to make eight pints of blueberry jam is a pretty cheap price to pay. Plus, I don't have to bend over, and they are all clean to boot.

Another favorite summer activity in Tanana was canoeing. Jerry and I bought a canoe the second year we moved out there. Now canoeing season is short since you can only do it while the river is running, and summers in Alaska are notoriously brief. Many times we'd just hop in the canoe after I got home from school and take a picnic over to a nearby sandbar and eat our dinner and just paddle around for a while. We had a little seven-horse motor for the canoe, and the river speed was probably about five miles per hour. Since we could only travel seven miles per hour, coming back upstream was kind of slow progress, but it was fun. During our time in the village, I think we explored all the sloughs, and in doing so, we saw a good part of the undeveloped country around Tanana. Sloughs (pronounced *slews*) are creeks or streams but are more shallow.

One year, we took our canoe upriver to Twelve-Mile, which was Patty and David Bowen's fish camp. It took us three hours to get up there, but we had a wonderful time and a nice visit, and going back was a piece of cake. We stopped at all the little tributaries that flowed into the Yukon and explored them as well. Now this was in the middle of summer, yet many of these small streams were still glaciated, so that was kind of interesting and also cool and refreshing.

One year, the day after Thanksgiving, we decided to visit Twelve-Mile. In the winter, we could travel on an all-terrain vehicle because there was an ice trail right on the river. So we started out and were about six miles into our journey. I remember thinking, *I wish I were shopping*. I had just seen a news story about how the day following Thanksgiving was the biggest shopping day of the year, and there I was out in this miserable cold weather, half freezing to death. (I don't even like to shop.)

When you drive an ATV, you have to press the gas button with your thumb, so your thumb is always cold because, although it's in your mitt, it's not next to your other fingers, where it could stay warm. Besides all that, we were traveling smack into the wind, so my forehead felt like it was permanently frozen.

When we finally got to the Bowens', they had a big fire in their fireplace, and it sure felt good to go inside and cozy up to it. But Jerry didn't want to stay too long because he was afraid the three-wheelers would freeze up, so we stayed just long enough to have some hot chocolate and to talk a little, and then we started back. The only good thing was, we didn't have to face the wind going back.

It was always fun to go up to the Bowens' camp. It was located in an especially beautiful sheltered spot out in the middle of nowhere.

They had built a lovely two-story log cabin and a log cabin sauna and bathhouse, which was situated right over their creek. So you could go in there and warm up and then go out into the creek and cool off. We tried that on several occasions when we visited, and it was very pleasant.

They also had the most beautiful outhouse view I've ever seen, and I've seen a lot of outhouses living here in Alaska. Theirs was set a little way away from their cabin, and it didn't have a door on it, so what you looked at, as you sat upon the throne, was a gorgeous vista of the Yukon River with snow-capped mountains in the background. It was outstanding.

CHAPTER 41

I N 1987 JERRY BOUGHT AN old 1947 pickup truck to drive around town in. It had been very well used, and the door didn't latch, so you had to strap yourself in with a bungee cord so the door stayed closed. Some of the floorboards were gone, so we put a red carpet in to cover up the hole in the floor. But we tooled around town in it, and it provided us lots of entertaining times. I remember when Sally and Bud came up to visit, Sally and I rode in the back and sat on upside-down milk crates. We waved to all the people in town as we passed them.

There were not a lot of places to drive to, but I remember we would go out to the dump in the pickup to see the "dump bear," who frequented the place and scavenged through the garbage.

The first time I saw a bear in Tanana, I was sitting at the table in our trailer, eating breakfast. I looked out the window, and a big black bear was lumbering through our yard. I was startled, astounded, and I was also scared. I jumped up and made sure the door was locked, and a thought crossed my mind, *A lot of good that's going to do.* If that bear had really wanted to rip the door off, it wouldn't have made a difference how many locks I had on it.

As I watched, I realized he was just using our yard as a shortcut to someplace else. Even so, it was kind of scary. That happened in the spring, so Jerry had already left for Wrangell to prepare our boat for the summer season. Needless to say, I didn't go outside alone too much after that. I remember I purposely did not go out to the store that day because I didn't know where that bear might be lurking.

Another time, I spotted a bear in the village. It was what the natives called a bad bear year. Because there wasn't any food up in the hills, the bears were coming right down into town to forage, and there had been numerous bear sightings. I had driven my four-wheeler to my friend Mary Starr's house, and we'd had a nice visit.

When I got back on my vehicle to leave, the town policeman was passing the house in his truck and asked me where I was going. I told him I was going home and pointed off the direction I was taking. He advised me not to take that route since a bear had been sighted down that way. He told me instead to go out and around to Front Street and then go down Front Street over to our place. I remember thinking how anybody could be sure the bear was going to stay in any one place. By that time, it could be over on Front Street.

Well, I hightailed it home, and although there was a speed limit in Tanana, that day I paid no attention to it. I did see the bear on my way home when it ran across the street in front of me and ran off into some bushes. I stepped on the gas and barreled right on by and home as fast as I could go.

The police officer ended up shooting the bear on the porch of the trailer Jerry and I owned, but it was standing empty at that time. I always harbored a little bit of healthy fear after that because there was no doubt about it—bears were a clear and present danger in Tanana.

We bought our first three-wheeler while we lived in Tanana. It was just a small one, but we had the best time with it. Well, one was fun but we figured if we each had a machine we could have twice as much fun, so we bought another. Not many days went by when we were not out exploring someplace.

In the spring, sometimes with snow still up to our armpits, we would take a coffee can and some fire-making supplies and hop on our ATVs and tool out into the woods, make camp, and fix tea. Or we might just wander out on the many trails around town. We always tried to take advantage of the weather while it was nice.

Then one winter, we bought a snow-go, and it turned out to be a piece of junk. I didn't like it because it was never reliable. First of all, you had to have a lot of upper body strength because it was a pull start. It seemed like every time I was operating the snow-go, it stalled out, and I could never get it restarted. It just made me so mad. Then I'd call Jerry, and he'd walk over to wherever I was stranded and get the darn thing started, usually on the first pull.

To make life a little easier on himself, Jerry built a sled to pull on the back of the machine, and he'd drive and pull me behind, standing on the sled. It was a racing sled, the kind serious dog racers used. Well, we made good use of that. We set out on it to find and cut our Christmas tree every year, and other times, we'd just follow one of the many dog trails around town and go for a ride. We saw a lot of country that way. We had to be picky, though, and not venture out when the weather was really frigid. So we were limited and found it was best to go if the temperature was zero or above. We did enjoy doing that, but after Jerry died, I sold the snow machine and never replaced it. It just wouldn't have been the same without him.

CHAPTER 42

Now in Tanana, during our second year there, the Catholic sisters, Sister Monique and Sister Maria, came to town. The sisters were originally from Belgium, and they had been down in St. Mary's, a little town on the Kuskokwim River, near Bethel. They had been on assignment there, teaching for thirteen years, before being transferred to Tanana.

They were two of the nicest, sweetest women I'd ever met, and we soon became very good friends. Since they were in service to the Catholic church in Tanana, it wasn't long before they extended an invitation to me to go to a Sunday worship service. During the service, I was allowed to participate in their Communion sacrament, but I had always been told that Catholic Communion was a closed service. The fact that I could be included changed the way I viewed Catholicism. I think being out in the middle of nowhere, like we were, helps people to become more ecumenical and open and to look past the lines of religious denominations.

The sisters stayed in Tanana for fourteen years, and it was fun to have them in the village. I know I really enjoyed them and learned a lot from them, and I know others did too. They now live in Fairbanks, and I still visit with them occasionally.

In the fall of 1989, we bought some land in Tanana located on Third Street, just behind the school playground. It was a pleasant wooded lot that two former Tanana teachers had owned before they moved away. The lot was empty when we bought it, so Jerry set about clearing it off and put in a pad, and we brought our own trailer so we wouldn't have to rent anymore. The trailer was eight by forty feet, and we bought it in Nenana and had it barged downriver to Tanana.

Well, we got it all set up on its pad, and then Jerry built on the side of it a wanigan, a small lean-to storage space that we definitely needed. It turned out very nice, almost nicer than the trailer itself. We cleaned our new home up. Jerry did the outside, and I washed the inside. We bought a new table and chairs, a new double bed, a new refrigerator, a couple of La-Z-Boys, and we even put in a wood-burning stove. By Halloween of that year, our new home was ready for us to move into.

It was a little more crowded and cramped than we were used to, but it was all ours. There was no running water, so it didn't have a flush toilet. It did have a bathroom in it with a toilet and a tub, so we put a plastic bag in the toilet and were able to use it at night instead of going outside to the outhouse.

Now I don't know if you've ever used an outhouse when it's cold outside, but that is not my idea of fun. We did use it during the day unless the temperature was more than fifty degrees below zero.

Jerry rigged the bathroom up so we could take showers, and the water just drained out into a big ditch outside the house. I learned it was possible to take a shower in just five gallons of water, and that included washing my hair. But I was only allowed to take a shower every other day. The first night in our new home, I took a shower at about seven o'clock in the evening, and my hair was still wet when I went to bed. In the morning, I was frozen to the wall by my hair and stuck there until Jerry came to my rescue. He thought it was very funny. I quickly learned to take my shower when I got home from school so my hair would be dry before bedtime.

I had very long hair at that time, and five gallons of water was not really enough to wash my body and my hair plus rinse out the conditioner, so I solved that problem by not using any conditioner. That posed another problem—it took about an hour to comb the tangles out of my hair. So my long hair didn't last very long. I had it all whacked off, and what a joy that was. I could really take a shower with only five gallons of water.

Now to operate the shower, we had a black shower bag that hung inside the stall, and we filled that with water. Then we removed enough to fill a teakettle and heated it to boiling and poured it back into the shower bag—instant hot shower. When the bag was empty, the shower was over. There was a valve to stop the water flow, so it didn't have to run continuously. The routine was this: get yourself wet, soap up, rinse off, and then just enjoy whatever water was left in the bag.

Despite the inconveniences, I really liked living in our own home. It was comfortable, it was in town, it was handy to the school, and it was all ours. Every day Jerry chopped wood for our stove and hauled our water supply. Except for the days we took our showers, we managed to live on about ten gallons of water a day.

CHAPTER 43

THE FIRST YEAR WE LIVED in our trailer, we found out that the electric oven in the stove didn't work, and because we moved in October, it wasn't possible to have a replacement shipped in on the barge because the river was already frozen over. So everything I cooked had to be cooked either on top of the stove or in my electric frying pan. I learned how to bake pies, cakes, and even cookies in an electric frying pan. I wouldn't suggest this to anybody who didn't need it, but it did work, and we survived. In the spring, we ordered a new stove. Oh my, I thought I'd died and gone to heaven; it was so fancy. Well, I thought it was fancy. It was just a simple four-burner apartment-size stove, but I loved it.

We also put up a walled tent for use as a garage for our four-wheeler and extra storage space for boxes and garden tools, so that left the wanigan free for Jerry to use as a workshop. He had a workbench and shelves for even more storage if needed. It was a little crowded, but like I said, it was all ours, and we were happy.

It was hard for us to move from a place that had running water to one that had none, but it wasn't impossible. However, let me just add now that I've been there, done that, and wouldn't want to do it again. I'm completely happy with my running water—good, clean running water.

One of the years while we lived in that trailer, we had a flood in the village. And wouldn't you know, it was May of 1991. Jerry had already left Tanana to start driving cross-country to Michigan with Mitch. The plan was, I would fly in to meet him there when school was out. Meanwhile, the Yukon River, being swollen with the spring thaw, was about to overflow its banks.

There were flood warnings out, and the water was already up on Front Street. School was dismissed early so we could go home to prepare for what was to come. I didn't have the first notion of what to do since I'd never experienced a flood before, but those who had been in the village for a while were only too glad to tell me what it would be like. They described, almost gleefully, other flood years when huge ice chunks from the thaw accompanied the dirty water, which rose steadily until dry land was impossible to find.

The first thing I did was to haul the canoe over next to the door and tie it to the steps in case I had to float out of there. I positioned the three-wheeler so all I had to do was hop on and roll out the door. I crammed a plastic bag full of everything I could possibly imagine needing—including all our important papers and documents—so if I had to head up to the hills, I could just grab it and go. I moved everything we owned up as high as I could get it onto counters and high shelves. I tried to protect anything of sentimental value for Jerry or me.

I remember distinctly it was on my birthday, May 6, when the water finally crested, and when it did, it just kept coming up, up, up, carrying with it a huge sheet of ice from the Yukon River, which was forcefully propelled down Front Street, wiping out all the trees in its path. I wasn't prepared for the devastation. It was horrible, and giant chunks of ice were lodged in people's front yards.

The good news was, the water never got back as far as our place because, keep in mind, we lived on Third Street. But the families who lived on First Street were very frightened because the ice chunks in their yards were six to ten feet thick. Ice that substantial can do some serious damage especially when it comes through with the force of an earthmover, having no respect for anything that might be in its way. There had been so many trees lining the banks of the river in Tanana, but the ice ripped most of them completely out. It was a very sad time for the village.

Another flood I remember was in 1994 on Mother's Day. There was a big ice jam downriver just above the town of Ruby, and the weather service was predicting the water would rise. Well, the river did rise, and I had never seen it that high. It was higher than it was when the ice broke up. This was after breakup, so this was just flowing water without any ice chunks, and it just kept coming up.

Soon it overflowed the banks and came up over the road that led to the airport. The Tanana fireman drove all around town in the fire truck, shouting, "Please get to higher ground. The Yukon River is ready to flood. Happy Mother's Day!"

So I went over and checked it out, and sure enough, the river was really high. So once again, I got my belongings together and got ready to evacuate if I should need to. There was a lot of water in front of Terry's Store, and it was flooded in front of the post office. Those were the two lowest spots on Front Street. Fortunately, the water began to recede, and for the second time, I was spared from having to evacuate.

During flood stage, the mood of the village was varied. Some people were scared, some were intrigued, and some, who had lived in Tanana a long time, were just passive about the whole thing. Their feeling was that every year the ice jammed up and the river got high but then nothing ever happened.

Those who were scared were either the very young, like my students, or the elderly. I think the children were afraid because they had never seen anything like it before. And the older generations were anxious because they had seen the destruction a flood could cause. One of the older native ladies, my friend Josephine, told me she remembered living in a house built on high pilings when one year the water came up so high ice chunks were grating on the underside of the house. She was fearful something like that could happen again.

Then there were those who were morbidly fascinated by the whole process. The water was already over the road leading out to the airport. The water was over a low spot in the road near Terry's Store. These people watched as the ice came up further and further. As it advanced, it pushed aside trees, boats, and outbuildings. The pressure build-up behind it was so great that when it cleared the bank, it just mowed down everything unlucky enough to be in its path.

So those intrigued individuals ventured out to find out what was going to happen next, and those at the other end of the spectrum, who were panic-stricken, packed up and were ready to get to the higher parts of town. Many of those who were most afraid lived in "the circle," which was a particularly low area where the HUD houses were built, and those homeowners had already made arrangements to evacuate to the school when the water got up that far. What they hadn't thought of yet was that if "the circle" flooded, the school would also be underwater.

Although the village was divided into three groups with diverse concerns, they all cared about one another and, in particular, the elderly, who were residents of the Elder's Home. The town revered its elders and had moved them to safety immediately when the flood was first predicted.

One of the things that impressed me about the people of Tanana was although they might not always see eye to eye with their neighbors, they always pulled together to help one another in emergencies. I think that's something good about small villages because you don't always experience that sense of togetherness in larger communities. But in Tanana, the feeling was very evident. The concern was not just for themselves; it was for the entire village

And they were definitely all worried about me because they all knew I was home by myself since Jerry and the dog had already left for the summer. They were ready to help with anything I needed. But I had already heeded their earlier warnings and moved everything in the house as high as it could go, and I would go with the neighbors up the Site Road if it became necessary.

I never got a feeling of apathy on the part of the people during that time either. These were people who didn't give up. They rolled with the flow. This was life. This was how it was on the river. They just seemed more able to handle things like a flood. Nobody liked it, but they were in tune with the weather, be it bitter cold or raging floods. No matter what came, they never lost hope, and they didn't lose faith. They all came together to help one another.

During the flood watch, there was always somebody out watching the river. It was the men's job to sit on the bank, watch, and report back so the people knew what was going on. We knew that when the bells of the Catholic and Episcopal churches tolled, it would mean, "Get the heck out!"

CHAPTER 44

S UMMER WAS A RELAXED, LAID-BACK time in the village, but in the late 1980s or early 1990s, the Tanana City Council decided they needed to teach all their kids how to swim. So they made a deal with the Campfire boys and girls to come out from Fairbanks and conduct swimming lessons in the river in a small sandy eddy. That turned out to be a bad idea since the river was very, very cold, so the city bought a huge round aboveground pool. It looked like a gigantic inflated raft measuring four feet deep, eight feet wide, and fifteen feet long. They set it up in the courtyard near the teachers' trailers, and that was a real treat.

The Campfire instructors came out and acted as lifeguards and also gave the kids lessons. The pool was open at certain hours, so adults could use it too. Every evening, Mary Starr and the sisters and I would go down and go swimming. What fun we had. The pool wasn't really big enough for adults to swim in, but it was just fun to be in the water and cool off because that was a very hot, hot summer.

When I moved back to teacher housing after Jerry died, the pool was right outside my door, and I loved that. And because I was an employee of the school district, I could use the pool whenever I wanted. Every night after dinner, Sandy Mangold and another neighbor and I took advantage of that privilege. Of course, in the summer, it stayed lit all night long, so we took advantage of that too. We had little rafts and all sorts of water toys. It was such a relaxing time. We could stay in as long as we wanted, and nobody even bothered us. The pool was a great addition to the town.

One summer, some neighbors decided to try their hand at gardening. They planted five rows of red, white, and blue potatoes and asked Sandy and me if we would like to help out. Now, I hate weeding and all that stuff, so I didn't help too much, but Sandy did. When it came time to harvest the potatoes, the people who had done the planting were on vacation for a month, so it fell to Sandy and me.

Well, there we were out digging potatoes, and I mean to tell you there must have been a million potatoes on one plant. These were huge potatoes. Some were red, some white, and some were blue. We dug and we dug and we got box after box after box of potatoes. We got to keep some because we helped. We harvested them in early September, and I was still eating potatoes in March.

Now let me explain about blue potatoes in case you're not familiar with them. They look gross because they're not only blue on the outside but they're also blue all the way through. I thought they tasted different. People told me I was crazy and that there was no difference in taste from any other potato, but they certainly didn't look appetizing. The red and white potatoes were marvelous. Some of them were huge. I wouldn't say they were as big as footballs, but they were darned close to it. One potato was enough for two or three meals for me, and I ended up giving a lot of my potatoes away to people in town.

It was interesting to me to watch things grow. Because of the long hours of daylight, growth was almost continual, and you could almost see the plants get bigger. Most of the flowers and vegetables grown in Alaska get to be huge in size and take big prizes for that at the various fairs.

CHAPTER 45

ANOTHER INTERESTING SKILL I LEARNED while I was in Tanana was how to make a marten hat. A marten is a small furry animal, highly prized because of its soft, glossy fur. Linda Swenson agreed to show me how to make a hat from the marten skins so I could surprise Jerry with it. I started in November by buying the skins, and I paid thirty dollars for the three skins required to make one hat. Then I had to learn how to tan the skins, but Linda showed me how to do that too.

Interestingly enough, a marten's hide is one of the easiest to tan. First, combine a mixture of two parts mayonnaise and one part milk, and spread it on the skin side of the hides. Roll them very tightly, and put them in a cool place for about twenty-four hours. Then wash them gently in Ivory Snow because that's mild, and then you have to work the hide with your hands and peel all the skin off the back of the pelt.

Well, by golly, I did it. I didn't have to chew it as Eskimo women would do with walrus and seal skins. I just worked it with my hands. There was a reddish cast to the fur, and when I got them all cleaned up, they looked beautiful.

Then Linda gave me her marten hat pattern, which had been handed down in her family from her grandmother, and she showed me how to carefully cut the pieces and sew them with dental floss to make the seams strong.

I surprised Jerry on Christmas, and he was so tickled to think I had done that for him. I was thrilled with the way the hat turned out for my first effort. A couple of years later, I made myself a hat, and we wore them for a long time. Just before he died, I made him another one because the first one had finally worn out. This time, the top of the cap was made with deer hide that Jerry's father had sent him, and it really turned out nice.

When Jerry died, that hat went with him. One of the many traditions in Tanana and the Athabascan culture is to dress the deceased body in the things they will need on their journey into the next life. I did eventually make myself another hat, and I still wear it now during the cold winters in Fairbanks.

A few years after I had mastered the marten hats, one of the native ladies in the village received a grant for Athabascan culture, and she was offering a class in skin sewing, so I went to her class and made a pair of mukluks. I needed a little extra help with them because my foot was so short and my calf was so fat that she had to get a special pattern.

The boots were made out of moose hide—and talk about tough sewing. That was some stiff stuff, but it was worth the effort, and they were really pretty when I was done. I trimmed them out with Arctic fox fur from several pelts Jerry had trapped in Savoonga. They really turned out pretty, and I was happy and satisfied with myself for having accomplished still another native skill. I wore them for several years, but when I left Tanana, I sold them to Pat White, and she was thrilled to get them.

I did enjoy learning the art of skin sewing. It was fun and very useful. I never did make any mitts for myself, but I did buy a pair of beaver mitts because they provide more warmth from the bitter cold than ordinary gloves or mittens. They flared out at the cuff so that my coat sleeve fitted down inside and air couldn't get in. I still have those, and they are on a braided yarn string, which is how all the people in the villages wear their mitts so they don't lose them when they need to take them off. For instance, you can't start a snow-go while wearing mitts. Then you just take them off, and they hang around your neck conveniently for getting them on again fast.

CHAPTER 46

E VERY YEAR IN THE FALL, an elderly lady named Grandma Effie Kokrine came to visit our school from Fairbanks. She was a native of Tanana and had lived in the village while growing up, so she had many stories of living in the wilderness long ago when she was a little girl. Usually, her visit coincided with our Tanana Week celebration.

Effie took us outside and showed the students how to make a shelter in the woods. She showed us how to use every part of a moose, how some of the sinew was used for a sandwich bag, and how the "piss bag" was cleaned out and used to haul water in. I don't think I'd want to drink out of it, but that was part of her story. The kids really enjoyed and looked forward to Effie coming each year, and they sat for hours, listening to her history come alive for them.

Usually during the winter, I included a snow lesson for the class and taught them how to build an igloo. That was really quite a chore because our snow in Tanana didn't work like Eskimo's snow—it wasn't hard and crunchy. But we managed to dig a hole and make a snow cave. Then I gave them all sorts of lessons like measuring the depth of the snow, finding out how cold it was at the top of the cave and how cold it was at the bottom. I showed them how to line a snow cave with willow and spruce branches to keep warm. It was always a fun lesson, but the class wanted something more. So one year, we went a little further. We thought that if people had a summer camp, there was no reason why we couldn't build ourselves a winter camp.

As a class, we had read the book *Winter Camp* by Kirkpatrick Hill, a woman author who lived in Ruby, one town downriver from Tanana. The book tells the story of two kids who survived in a winter camp with their grandmother after their father died suddenly. So my students decided they wanted to try setting up a winter camp themselves.

We found a spot not too far from the school between Third Street and Airport Road, and we set about making our winter camp. We wanted to have it done before it snowed so that we could get things in place. We dug a fire pit and moved in some benches around it, and then I divided the class into four groups. Each group had instructions to build some sort of a shelter that would keep them warm. I distributed to each group a roll of twine, and they could use hatchets and knives, but other than that, they had to build the shelter out of what was available to them.

I set it up as a contest, and we worked on them for at least three weeks. Some students used willow boughs to build with, while others strung their twine around the trees and bushes and then hung the branches on that. Still another group used twine to tie the willow boughs together first and then fastened them on the top of pieces of poles from trees to hold them up.

I wish you could have seen those shelters to appreciate the thought and ingenuity that went into them. When they were done, they held a contest, judged by the students to see whose shelter was the best constructed. When the camp construction was finished we held an open house and invited parents, the principal, and the school superintendent to a hotdog roast at our fire pit.

I had asked the shop teacher to make a tripod for us so that we could hang a pot of water over our fire to make tea and hot chocolate. So that was our menu, and for dessert, we made s'mores. It was a really great celebration, and the parents and school personnel had a good time and declared that the class had made a very fine winter camp.

Every week, we went out to our camp and spent time there. We made snares and actually snared rabbits and tanned the hides. We discovered that the skins of the rabbits in the interior of Alaska weren't very good for tanning because the hides were too thin. But we tanned them anyway and sent them to our pen pals in Hershey, Pennsylvania. The kids had a fun time with their winter camp and learned a lot at the same time. Sometimes we'd go out and build a big fire and have a hotdog roast for the fun of it. It was something to look forward to during the long, cold winter.

CHAPTER 47

S OMETIME DURING MY SECOND SPRING in Tanana (once again, Jerry was down at the boat), I ran out of laundry detergent, and I called my neighbor Jane Jackman to see if she had some she could spare.

She said, "Yes. But don't come out now."

"Why?"

"You haven't heard about the murders?"

"Murders? Where?"

It turned out there was a murderer up in Manley Hot Springs, and this person had shot thirteen people, hopped in a boat, and was floating downriver. They thought by now he should be someplace around Tanana. Well, that scared me pretty good, and I forgot about needing laundry detergent. When I got off the phone, my friend Linda Swenson called to say she was sending her daughter Stephanie over to stay with me so I wouldn't be alone. So Stephanie came over, and we waited.

Every house in the entire village was locked up tight, and eventually, the criminal was apprehended just outside our village. The state police, flying over the area in a helicopter, spotted him and shot and killed him. He was a homeless drifter that just came into town and started shooting people at random. It was horrible and very scary. You usually hear about things like that happening in other places but not in a quiet little bush village.

There were a few other times of scary excitement during the years I spent in Tanana. One day in 1994 or 1995, I was teaching in my classroom when the principal stopped at the door of my classroom and motioned for me to come out into the hallway. I thought it was strange since I was right in the middle of a lesson, but I did as he asked.

He told me he wanted me to close my classroom door and he was going to lock it from the outside. He said, "I don't want you or any of the kids to come out."

Now, I'm not the type to just do something like that without knowing why, and when I questioned him, he said, "Just do as I say. There's a man in the school, and he has a gun."

Well, that nearly sent me into hysteria because it was right around the time when school shootings in bigger cities of the Lower 48 were very much a part of daily newscasts. I couldn't believe it was happening in Tanana.

I did what the principal told me, and then I calmly announced to the class that we wouldn't be going out for recess today. Instead we would play some of their favorite inside games. The class saw nothing strange in that since we did it every now and then anyway.

I told them, "We need a lot of room in this classroom to move around and play the games. So we're going to move this big rolling cabinet over in front of the door." I figured a man with a gun could easily look through the window and shoot through it.

So we shoved the cabinet over to the door, and it effectively blocked the window. The kids still didn't suspect anything even when I said, "We're not going to take a bathroom break right now. We'll play and take a break afterward."

About an hour later, the principal came by and unlocked the door. He opened it and said, "Everything is okay." I could at last breathe easy, and the kids didn't learn the real story of the incident until sometime later.

It turned out there was another drifter in town. He had paddled down the Yukon in a canoe and, for some reason, decided to stay for a while in Tanana. So he was just hanging around and walking through the streets of town, armed with his gun. Before the incident at the school even took place, the police officer had warned the man he had to move on, and the man loaded up his belongings in his canoe and headed on downriver. Unfortunately, the ice had started running in the river, and he had returned to Tanana. The ice would have ripped out the bottom of his canoe, so he was stuck in the village until spring. Nobody liked the idea, but there was no choice.

He was living in a tent out at the campgrounds near the airport, and during the days, he roamed through town, always carrying his big rifle. He hung around the Laundromat or the school because they were warm places. The day he came into the school, waving his weapon around, our police officer contacted the state police, and troopers flew out in a helicopter and landed in the side yard of the school next to my classroom. They came into the school, captured the guy, and took him off in chains. I don't know what happened to him, and I really don't care, but that was pretty scary. After that, Tanana resumed its status as a quiet little village.

CHAPTER 48

WE HAD SEVERAL CHARACTERS IN town, and one of them was an outsider named Bill White. When my nephew Kevin visited me, he nicknamed Bill "Smiles with No Teeth" because, at that time, he didn't have his false teeth but always had a big smile for everyone. Bill was another drifter, but he ended up staying in Tanana and married a woman in town named Pat Bean. She was the school librarian and knew nothing of the man's history, but she fell in love with him, and they bought a place up on Mission Hill and, for a time, were quite happy.

Pat owned an old horse, the only horse in Tanana, so we really did have a "one-horse town." The horse's name was Doc, and after Pat and Bill married, they had three more horses shipped downriver from Fairbanks, so they had the only ranch in Tanana.

Then, one day the couple had a quarrel about who should be feeding the horses. Bill decided he didn't want to do it anymore, so he shot and killed one of them and left it right in the middle of the road to rot. Well, that prompted Pat to finally look into Bill's background. Now, his story was that he had been adopted and he didn't remember where he came from or anything about his childhood.

After some researching, Pat discovered the man she married was a Mohawk Indian from New York, so she decided she would try to locate his birth mother. At one point, Pat thought she had located the woman and invited her to visit Tanana. But the information Pat had was incorrect, so that meeting never took place.

Well, time went on, and Pat began to let it slip to some people that Bill was beating her. Besides that, she had a feeling that something wasn't right, and Bill's stories did not always mesh. And then the authorities stepped in and began checking into Bill White's past. It seemed Bill White wasn't really Bill White at all. Bill White was really Leroy something or other. Leroy had assumed someone else's identity, and he was running away from all sorts of tangled predicaments and scrapes from a previous life.

Leroy had an uncle whose name was Bill White, and his uncle had died. So Leroy married his uncle's wife, who was really his aunt and was quite a bit older than he was. Nobody ever knew the reason he married her, but when it didn't work out, he decided to just disappear. He gathered some gear, a canoe, a sleeping bag, and a few other necessities; drove to Whitehorse, where he left his car; got into his canoe; and floated away down the Yukon. And once he got into the river, in his mind, he was no longer Leroy. He had become Bill White. So when he arrived in Tanana, that was who he said he was. That was his story, and he stuck to it.

It was the little details that began to make Pat wonder about the man she'd married. He had two different Social Security numbers. He had two different birth dates, and it turned out he was wanted in several places on outstanding arrest warrants and had a long criminal record. When he finally took a job working for the weather observatory in Tanana, he was required to be fingerprinted, which started the descent to his eventual demise.

Leroy was sent back to New York to stand trial there, but the last I knew, he was also still wanted in Tanana for stealing from the FAA and the Department of Transportation. I doubt seriously if he will ever be back.

PART VI
SPECIAL AWARDS AND ENDINGS

WHEN I FIRST WENT TO Tanana in 1982, it was the first year the village operated as an independent school district. Our first superintendent was Bob Jackman. After Bob, there was a succession of superintendents, but one that stands out in my mind is Vince Barry. He was an older man and came to Tanana with his wife, Joanne. He stayed for five years and, during that time, was an inspiration to me. I absolutely loved him. He just was so into children and so into education, and it was very good for the school.

Vince made me believe in myself and showed me what I was doing was right on and that if I wanted to, I could teach wherever I wanted to teach. I truly enjoyed working with him mostly because he cared so much about the kids and that was his top priority. He brought the school district a long way in educational terms, and he was just a nice person besides. Vince Barry was the person who got me involved enough to receive the prestigious Milken Award, a twenty-five-thousand-dollar prize funded by the Milken family and bestowed on outstanding teachers to be used in any way they chose.

In the first year, the award was given to eight teachers in the state of California. The next year, it expanded into Nevada, and from there, it just started to grow. By 1989 when Alaska was included for the award, each participating state was allowed six recipients—three for elementary excellence and three at the high school level. A mix of men and women was required. One had to be a principal, and there had to be at least one representative from a minority. There was never a list of winning educators; instead the Milken people charged each individual state with unearthing their most unique and worthy recipients. There was no rhyme or reason as to how teachers were chosen, but somewhere, somehow their names came up, and the actual selection process was never revealed.

Well, it was in September of 1990, and Jerry had won himself a permit to hunt caribou in the hills above Ferry, down near Healy on the road system. So he had gone hunting and was going to be gone for a week with his friend Pi. I was teaching one afternoon, and I was right in the middle of a lesson when the principal, Richard Lee, came into my room.

He said, "Suzanne, you have a phone call."

I said, "Well, I'm in the middle of teaching."

But he insisted, "It's very important, and you need to take this phone call."

I asked, "Who is it?"

He said, "Just go take the phone call. I'll stay with your kids."

So I went down to the office, picked up the phone, and said in an impatient voice, "Hello! This is Suzanne Henning."

The voice on the other end of the phone identified herself as Sue Wilken, president of the state school board, and she said, "I just wanted to tell you that you have just been named to receive the Milken Award."

I said, "Yeah? Big deal."

She explained, "No. Really. This is the Milken Award, and it is a twenty-five-thousand-dollar cash award."

My exact words to her were "I am a teacher, and I don't think this is very funny. I am in the middle of teaching, and you are interrupting me. I have better things to do."

Hurriedly she tried to explain further. "No. No. This is real. Do you know about the Milken Award?"

"No."

So she patiently explained it to me again. By this time, I was beginning to believe her story must be true. And when I had first voiced my annoyance, she said, "That's kind of the reaction I got from the last person I called."

"There are other people?"

"Yes. There are six teachers in the state that have been selected for this award." She went on to tell me what I was going to receive and what it entailed. I would be going down to Anchorage for the state award, and then I would be going to Los Angeles for the national award ceremony.

Then she added, "You can't tell anyone yet because the names haven't been released to the press."

So I hung up and, still in a daze, went back to my classroom. I began to question Richard, "Do you know what that call was about?"

"Yes."

"So that woman said I was going to get twenty-five thousand dollars, but I think that must be wrong. That's a lot of money. She must have meant to say twenty-five hundred dollars."

"Well, I don't know about that. I just know you were selected for the award."

"How come you knew about it? I've never heard of it before."

"Because Vince Barry told me about it."

Vince was in his office, so I just barged in and said, "Vince."

He started to laugh. "I am so proud of you. This is just wonderful." Then he got right up and hugged me.

"She told me I couldn't tell anybody else."

"That's right. The only people that know are you, me, and the principal, and we'll just keep it until they release it to the press."

Now I'm thinking, *Right! This lady calls me up, tells me I've just won twenty-five thousand dollars, and I can't tell anybody?*

By this time, it was just about lunch hour, and when the kids filed out to go to the cafeteria, I went out the back door to go home for lunch, talking to myself all the way. *Suzanne, you just won twenty-five thousand dollars. You of all people! All you ever wanted to do was teach.*

So I was walking down the street, talking to myself, and there came the school maintenance man, Billy Sam, around the corner.

He looked at me and said with real concern in his voice, "Suzanne, are you all right?"

I assured him that everything was fine and added, "It's just been one of those days."

So he walked on, and I thought, *Here I am, acting like a lunatic. I have two of Billy Sam's boys in my class, and he thinks I'm crazy.*

When I got home, I talked to Mitch. "Mitch, I just won twenty-five thousand dollars."

Mitch nuzzled my leg but showed no other enthusiasm and didn't say a word. I kept trying to think of someone I could tell. I called Pi's house, but there was no answer, so I left a message: "Jerry, call me immediately. It's very important."

Then the thought crossed my mind—I could call my family. Well, I couldn't call Mom and Dad because they were in their motorhome on the road, traveling. So I decided I'd just call up my sister. I dialed her number, and my brother-in-law, Bud, answered and said she wasn't home. So I told Bud, and I thought, *You know, if he can get that back to Tanana before they release it in the newspaper, too bad because I had to tell somebody.*

Well, Bud was just as astounded and happy as I was, and I was glad to finally be able to share my news.

I went back to school, and of course, I was walking on cloud nine, thinking, *This can't possibly be happening. All my life, all I've ever wanted to be was the best that I could be at what I was doing. I never ever went into teaching with the thought that I would get an award for doing something that I so dearly love.*

I cry about it to this day. To think that out of all the millions and millions of wonderful teachers there were, I was chosen as one of six to receive this award for the state of Alaska. What a great honor!

From then on, when the award made its way into my conscious thought, I remembered that silly little girl with the long pigtails who used to sit in class and hung on every word the teacher said. And here she was winning an award for what was her whole life. I was just thrilled.

That afternoon, I tried to teach, but every time I thought about it, I was flabbergasted again. Twenty-five thousand dollars was a lot of money, and it was beyond belief. So I talked to my principal again. I called the lady back and asked if there was a mistake and if the award was maybe for twenty-five hundred dollars.

She said, "No, it is twenty-five thousand dollars, and it's yours to do with whatever you wish. It's your money. It's not for your classroom, and there are no restrictions on how you choose to spend it. It's just a way of thanking you for being a wonderful, marvelous teacher."

I still found it hard to believe. I managed to get through the rest of the day, and after school, the principal and the superintendent had to talk to me again because they were so tickled that I had won. And I was still on cloud nine. I just couldn't seem to quit grinning.

When I got home from school, Jerry called, and I asked him if he was sitting down.

"No, I can't sit down because I'm at a pay phone."

He was at the KOA campground, and he'd gotten the message that I had called. But Pi was using the phone at the house, so Jerry went down to KOA because he thought it sounded urgent.

I said, "Honey, I've won twenty-five thousand dollars for being a good teacher."

"Say what?"

So I repeated myself and told him it was the Milken Award.

He said, "I never heard of it."

"I've never heard of it either, but it's for real."

"Well, I wasn't going to come home for a couple more days, but I'll be home tomorrow."

By the next day it was okay for me to tell people, but I was a little hesitant to tell the people in town because I didn't like to toot my own horn. Mom and Dad had found out from Sally, and they called from the road to congratulate me.

Jerry came home the next day, and he still couldn't believe it. He called his parents to tell them, and of course, it went all through his family grapevine. I got all sorts of cards and letters and notes from people I hadn't heard from in a while. The school district held a potlatch to announce I had received the award, and everyone seemed truly excited that someone in the village was famous.

Later that week, I received a letter from the Milken Family Foundation, congratulating me and describing the award. I had to have my picture taken and sent in to them with a little blurb about my teaching experience. I was still so bewildered. I couldn't even think of anything to write, so my superintendent, Vince Barry, wrote it for me.

When Sue Wilken first called me, I asked her how I was chosen for the award. She said that information was never disclosed, but she did tell me it was not just one person that submitted a name.

"We interviewed many people you have taught and worked with."

When I told that to Jerry, he said, "Since you don't know whom they called and whom they didn't, you're going to have to be nice to everybody!"

About a year later, Vince Barry said to me, "You know, they interviewed me, and I talked on the phone for an hour and a half or two hours, telling them all the wonderful and marvelous things you do for children."

I started to cry. It's overwhelming to think how deeply I touched other people's lives when all I ever wanted to do was just to teach. I never found out the names of anyone else the foundation interviewed, but I would like to thank them now, publicly, for their kind words and approval of my work.

It's my theory that my name probably got into their files for the award because I had gone through the Math Consortium and started doing in-services within the state. Not only in math, but I had also been doing in-services in reading because of having my master's degree as a reading specialist. I guess I'll never know for sure, but I'm still grateful.

CHAPTER 50

I

N OCTOBER JERRY AND I were flown, all expenses paid, from
Fairbanks to Anchorage. I remember we had to stop in Fairbanks
and buy Jerry a sport coat because he had to dress up and he
didn't have a decent jacket.

We were staying at the Anchorage Hilton Hotel, and we were
wined and dined in great style. Since this was the first time the award
had ever been presented in the state, they seemed to want to go all
out.

First of all, when we got to the room, I found a little tin mailbox
with a big welcome sign on it, and out of it was flowing candy and
nuts and oranges like a cornucopia. It was from the hotel, and the
accompanying card read: "Welcome. You are special, and we're so
proud that you're staying here with us."

The hotel had also placed a huge bouquet of flowers in the
room. There was also a telegram from my sister with congratula-
tions and telling me how proud she was of me. If I had it to do over,
I would have wanted my family there to share in the celebration
because that was, in my estimation, one of the most important events
that happened in my life.

I had to be interviewed by the Milken Family Foundation,
which sent its own videography team from Los Angeles to tape the
interview. A reception on the top floor of the Hilton was held in
honor of Alaska's six award winners. There was a huge wraparound
window in the room, and I remember it was an absolutely gorgeous
day. There were all sorts of hors d'oeuvres and beverages at the reception, and one thing I do remember quite clearly is that I was wearing
shoes that hurt my feet. And the dress I was wearing was the one I
had worn to my niece's wedding.

The actual awards banquet was held downstairs in the main
dining room. The room was all decorated, and there were special

tables for the awardees to sit at, so we were all up in front. Other people at our table included my principal, my superintendent, and a state school board member.

Other award winners that year were Grace Ann Heacock (Fairbanks, third grade), Dora Kline (Dillingham, bilingual classes), Larry Moye (Barrow, high school math teacher), Paul Sucher (Anchorage, elementary school principal), and Paul Bower (Petersburg, high school science teacher). They were the nicest people to get to know, and this banquet was in our honor. Sometimes it was hard to grasp that thought. Alaska state senators and the governor himself, Walter J. Hickel, were in attendance. It was just a huge celebration—and all because I wanted to be a teacher.

After a wonderful dinner, the program began, and the emcee was the editor of the *Anchorage Daily News*. He called each one of us up to the podium individually and alphabetically, and we were each expected to give a speech. Now, no one had mentioned that I would have to speak in front of a large audience, so it was lucky for me my last name began with *H* and I was the third person introduced. That gave me a little extra time to figure out what I would say.

Looking back, I'm glad they didn't tell me I would be making an acceptance speech because I would have worried and fretted over it, and I certainly wouldn't have been able to enjoy any other part of the celebration and ceremony. So when I began to speak, what I had to say came from my heart. I remember saying there were several reasons I had gotten to where I was and the three biggest reasons were my mom, my dad, and my husband. And of course, I started to cry then because Dad really did encourage us to go to school even though he only completed eighth grade. I can't remember all I said, but it was one of those things that really came from my heart, and there were so many ifs. If it hadn't been for this or that, I wouldn't have been where I was, but I was there, and I just had so many people to thank for it.

I didn't receive the twenty-five thousand dollars because that first observance was at the state level. The money would be awarded when I attended the national ceremony in March of 1991.

CHAPTER 51

ELL, MARCH CAME, AND AGAIN both Jerry and I were flown, all expenses paid, for an award-winning week in Los Angeles, California. We stayed at the Beverly Hilton Hotel in Beverly Hills, California. Talk about class. This was top of the line, and we didn't even have matching luggage. Jerry had a duffel bag, and I had a crummy old suitcase I had been using since I graduated from high school.

Mom and Dad drove over to LA in their motorhome from their winter quarters in Boulder City, Nevada, and parked someplace outside the city and came up and stayed with us at the hotel. Our room was huge and had three telephones, one by the bed, one on the desk, and another in the bathroom. We were on the first floor in what they described as a garden room, and we had a door that actually opened onto a garden.

One evening, Jerry was standing out in the garden, smoking when some Secret Service men approached him. They accused him of "lurking" in the bushes. It seemed that, at that very time, President Reagan was in town to meet with Lech Walesa of Poland and both of them were staying at the Beverly Hilton. Consequently, the grounds were crawling with Secret Service personnel, and they had identified Jerry as a suspicious person.

After we settled in, I discovered I literally had nothing to wear. I mean, we were talking fancy here, and nothing I brought, or even owned, was going to work. So I went out and started buying clothes. I found a dress I absolutely loved. The price tag was ninety-six dollars, making it the most expensive article of clothing I had ever owned, but I fell in love with it. I remember, after the celebration dinner and speeches were over and we got back to the room, I noticed the price tag was still hanging out the back of it. I was really glad that I had stood at the beginning of the line, so I was in the back when everybody got up on stage. I hoped nobody else had seen it. Minnie Pearl came to mind.

They fed us like kings and queens. There were big breakfasts and wonderful lunches and all sorts of meetings with food, and every night there was a big banquet. The officials made Mom and Dad feel so welcome. They had tickets to the award banquet, and they even attended a predinner reception for the Alaska winners with me.

One of the things I remember is, we had to get in line first alphabetically by states and then, within the states, alphabetically by our last names. The man who was passing out the twenty-five-thousand-dollar checks was called away for a minute, and he said to me, "Here hold this." And he shoved a fat packet into my hand. So I was holding all the checks for all the state winners. I have never held that much money since, and I doubt if I ever will again.

The Milken Family Foundation was governed by a board of directors, and at that time, the board included Roosevelt Grier, a former NFL star lineman turned television and movie star, and Dennis Weaver from TV's *Gunsmoke*. I met both of them and had my picture taken with them. Rosie Grier and his wife expressed an interest in Alaska, so I invited them to come to Tanana. Of course, they never did, but I did extend the invitation.

While I was in LA for the award ceremony, I met the recipients from Michigan, my home state. It was, and still is, always a treat to meet someone from "home." I met a lot of neat and interesting people from all over the United States, at least from the thirteen states represented that year. The program has now grown to include all fifty states, whose teachers compete for the Milken Award.

While we were in sunny California, we strolled down Rodeo Drive. Jerry had planned to buy a special gift for me from him to commemorate the occasion, so later while I was attending one of my meetings, he returned to Rodeo Drive to a fancy jewelry store, Van Cleef & Arpels, with the idea of buying me a beautiful gold barrette for my hair.

As he entered the store, he was met at the door and promptly escorted out. They said he didn't fit their image of a customer, dressed as he was in his jeans and his new flannel shirt. So he said if his money wasn't good enough, he'd just take his business elsewhere. And he did, and I still have that lovely barrette to this day. Later we went back and snapped a picture of Jerry and Mom standing in front of the jewelry store that threw him out.

In our room, we could make unlimited phone calls, and room service was provided at any time of the day or night. It seemed like the Milken people had anticipated our every need, and we wanted for nothing. I had never been treated quite that royally before and probably never will be again, but it sure was fun while it lasted.

I decided, before my fifteen minutes of fame at the ceremony, I would get my hair done, a luxury I hadn't splurged on in quite a while. I made an appointment with a salon located in the hotel, and at the arranged time, Mom and I went to the shop. A receptionist whisked me into the depths of the salon and introduced me to a male hairdresser, who just took over and seemed to know what he was doing.

When I emerged forty-five minutes later, Mom's mouth fell open in obvious shock, and I started to cry. My hair looked terrible. It was really, really big, and I looked like I belonged in a sixties-style girl singing group.

On the way back to the room, Mom was trying really hard not to laugh, and I didn't even try not to cry—I sobbed like a baby. When we walked in the door, Jerry said, "My God! You could have gotten that for free by sticking your finger in an electrical outlet." Then the dam burst, and I cried harder.

The time was four-thirty, and we had to be at the first reception of the evening at five-thirty, so I jumped in the shower. The steam started rolling out, and in an effort to get over my anger, I scrubbed my skin clean. When I finally came out and dared to look in the mirror again, the steam had quieted the hair down a little, and it didn't look half bad. I was pleased, and I was really glad I'd thought to get in the shower.

That night at the ceremony, I received my check, and I had my picture taken with it because you don't know when you'll ever get another check for twenty-five thousand dollars. The honor of receiving the Milken Award didn't stop there either. I was invited back every year for the next five years to the LA presentation and the National Educator Award. And the Milken Foundation always paid for my travel and other expenses. Mom and Dad were always in Boulder City at that time, so they always took the time to come and share the week with me in California.

CHAPTER 52

G ETTING HOME AGAIN PROVED TO be an adventure in itself. When we left LA for home on Sunday, we flew via Seattle, where we had a layover, then finally boarded and took off. There were two college hockey teams on our plane, and two players from opposing teams, who were sitting right across the aisle from me, got into a fight. I was seated in the aisle seat, and Jerry was next to the window with an empty seat between us. All of a sudden, I felt a hand grab the back of my collar and pick me up and push me out of the way of the two guys who, by this time, were really landing some serious blows to each other.

Finally, the pilot came back. The team coaches came from their first-class seats, and they managed to restrain the two players. Shortly after that, a voice over the loudspeaker announced the plane would be making an emergency landing in Vancouver, BC, to let some passengers off. Can you just imagine those phone calls?

"Hey, Mom, can you send some money? I just got thrown off the plane in Canada."

I never found out what happened to the two boys, but our plane took off again, and we flew into Anchorage with no more incidents. However, when we landed at the Anchorage airport, we were informed the crew was too tired to fly any farther and that was as far as the plane was going that night.

By that time, it was two o'clock in the morning, and they just put us off the plane. Well, I marched up to the reservation desk and said, "Now look here! We have to have a room." You need to know that, at that time, the Anchorage airport folded up at night. I mean, there was nothing open there at all unlike Chicago or other big cities where flights were scheduled all night long.

Airline personnel informed us they couldn't provide a room for us, so we slept as much as possible in the airport waiting room and caught the first available flight to Fairbanks at six o'clock the next morning. Flight personnel announced a major snowstorm in Fairbanks, but the plane would take off. We later learned ours was the only plane that landed in Fairbanks that day because the snow never stopped.

After we collected our bags in the Fairbanks airport, we couldn't get a taxi right away because the snow was really deep and vehicles were having a really hard time of it. So there we were with our big suitcases, no winter coats and no boots. We had left them at the motel when we left for LA because we knew we wouldn't need them there. We finally did flag a taxi down, but it couldn't quite make it all the way to our motel because of the huge drifts. So we got out at the nearest corner, Jerry slogged over to the motel for our coats and boots, and we managed to get into them. From there, the taxi driver took us to Gabe's Auto Service, where we'd left our truck to be serviced while we were gone. Again, the driver couldn't quite make it down the little side road all the way to Gabe's, so we were dropped off at the nearest corner.

Jerry said, "Okay, you stand here with the suitcases, and I'll walk down and get the truck."

The truck was a four-wheel drive, so we knew he could get that out. So I stood there on the corner in Fairbanks with snow up to my armpits, and I thought, *I sure wish I had a camera, so I could send the Milken Foundation a picture of their award winner trying to get home.* Just the night before, I had been wined and dined in splendor and had a check in my purse for twenty-five thousand dollars, and the next day, I was stranded on a corner, in a blizzard, with my suitcases piled around me. It was a humbling experience, and I had to laugh, or I might have cried.

Jerry finally came with the truck, and we were able to get all the way into the motel parking lot, but we had to stay another night in Fairbanks since nobody was flying to Tanana because the weather was so bad.

When we at last got home, the adventure continued. We had to dig down to get into our trailer because the snow was so deep. Instead of going up four steps to our porch, we had to go down four snow steps to get into our front door. I don't think I have ever been so glad to be home as I was that day—tired but happy.

The second year I attended the Milken Awards was not nearly as stressful traveling. I stayed at the Century Plaza Hotel and Towers in LA, and it was pretty fancy too. Mom and Dad came again and stayed with me. They had never ordered room service, so one morning when I had to attend a breakfast meeting, before I left, I ordered breakfast to be sent up for them. They were tickled to be pampered that way and talked about it for a long time afterward.

Each year I attended I had a really fun time, and it seemed like something new and different happened every time. I am especially grateful for the opportunities I had to meet so many wonderful people from all around the United States.

CHAPTER 53

During my time in Tanana, I received another prestigious honor: the Presidential Award for Excellence in Science and Mathematics Teaching. This was an award given once a year by the president of the United States to four teachers of math and science from each state, two at the elementary level and two from high school.

In September of 1992, I received notification that I had been chosen as one of the teachers to be given this award. One evening I got a call from a friend of mine who was teaching in Ketchikan and had received the Milken Award. He called to congratulate me for being singled out for the Presidential Award, but I hadn't gotten word of it yet. He had received the high school level math award, and when he got his letter, the other winners were listed. My letter hadn't yet arrived.

The next day in school, I had scheduled our annual field trip for Tanana Week. We were out in the middle of a field, digging a fire pit in the sand, when I saw Jerry's truck come bumping down the dirt road. The truck skidded to a stop, and Jerry jumped out, waving an official-looking envelope at me.

"Hey! Just thought you might like to have this. It's a letter from the White House."

Sure enough, it was my letter from President Clinton, congratulating me on receiving the 1993 Presidential Award, and I was pretty excited. My class cheered wildly as I announced it to them even though they didn't quite grasp the enormity of it all. What that award meant for me was, aside from the prestige, there was also the seven thousand five hundred dollars in prize money to spend in my classroom for the enhancement of the math and science programs in any way I saw fit. The letter was also an invitation to go to the White House the following April for all the pomp and circumstance involved in the presentation of the award. To say I was thrilled would be an understatement.

Jerry said the actual event was going to be too hoity-toity for him, so he chose not to go with me. But he suggested I ask my sister, Sally, who was almost as thrilled as I was to be going to Washington, DC.

So on a warm spring day in May of 1993, I flew into Chicago's O'Hare airport and met up with my sister. We had devised a way to find each other in the teeming terminal. I sent her an Alaska T-shirt with chubby little Eskimo ladies on the front, and I would be wearing a matching shirt. I figured they were distinctive enough that if Sally and I didn't find each other maybe someone would remark they had seen another woman wearing the same shirt. As it turned out, we passed each other on a moving walkway and got off at our next stop and hurried to board another plane together bound for the nation's capital.

When our plane landed, there to meet us at the airport were Mom, Dad, and Sally's son, my nephew Kevin. Mom and Dad had driven their motorhome from Las Vegas, stopped in Ohio to pick up Kevin, and were parked in a campground in Maryland. They had come to Washington DC for the festivities and to make it a real family affair.

Sally and I couldn't check into our assigned hotel until the next day, so we found a hotel for the night with two adjoining rooms, and it was really fun to have some of my family there to share my excitement.

The next morning, we discovered something was the matter with Mom and Dad's car, so we had to take it to a gas station for repairs. I remember we went to eat breakfast, and then we sat in a gazebo in a pretty little park and waited for the car to be fixed. By the time we picked it up, it was time for Sally and me to go to our hotel. So Mom, Dad, and Kevin delivered us to the Omni-Shoreham Hotel right in downtown DC, and we were able to check in. We had a spacious room with a nice view and lots of closet space for all the clothes we brought with us.

There were many events scheduled in the awardees' honor—dinner dances, a fifties dance, a dinner in the State Department dining room. Oh my, they fed us like kings and queens, and events were scheduled for our traveling companions to coincide with meetings that the honorees had to attend.

While we were there, my family and I went shopping at the Pentagon Mall in Maryland, and it was huge. We took the subway there and were amazed at how easy the subway system in DC was to use. We visited the Smithsonian Institution Museum of Space and Flight and walked on the Capitol Mall. We even took Mom and Dad to the Hard Rock Café at Kevin's request and had a great time.

One day during some free time, Sally and I decided to visit the Vietnam Memorial, which neither of us had seen. So we took the subway by ourselves and did really well. When we got to our stop and walked upstairs to street level, we saw a man selling watches, which he pinned to the underside of his overcoat, and he whipped it open to show us. Being true tourists, we each bought a watch. Sally's lasted for several years; mine died before we got back on the subway for the return trip. It just needed a new battery! What can you expect for nine dollars and ninety-nine cents?

Since we didn't know where the monument actually was, we decided to take a taxi and then discovered we had only been three blocks away and could have walked. The Vietnam Memorial was awesome. With the help of the name locator, I was able to locate a friend, Al Gomez, whom I had gone to high school with, and that was a very moving experience.

One evening, all the recipients and their guests were invited to a dinner cruise on Chesapeake Bay, and what a nice time that was. Then on Thursday of that week, I received my award in a morning ceremony held in the Samuel P. Langley Theater. Mom, Dad, Kevin, and Sally were present for that also. It really meant a lot to me that my family would come clear across the country to see me receive an award, an award that seemed like a bonus for all the wonderful times I had in my teaching career.

I took the seven thousand dollars and bought several things for my classroom to enhance not only my math program but all my other courses as well. I bought a video camera and a laptop computer. I got a whole set of thirty-six calculators for the kids to use. I purchased several different math manipulatives and an overhead projector.

I used the video camera to tape some of the things the class was doing math-wise in the classroom so the programs could be passed on to other schools in the state. And when I finally left teaching, since those items had been purchased with my own money, I was able to pass on the video camera to my niece, and I gave the laptop to Mom. The calculators I left for a new teacher in Tanana so that part of my award continued to be used even after I retired.

CHAPTER 54

On September 26, 1993, Jerry died unexpectedly, and that was a really hard time for me. Sandy Mangold, my neighbor, graciously opened her home to me, and people came to be with me all through the night as well as the next day. They brought in food, and the older native ladies in the village came to sew clothes for Jerry for his journey into the hereafter, according to traditional Athabascan culture. I asked the ladies if it would be appropriate for me to include the marten hat I had made for him, and they said it certainly would. One lady made some beaded gloves, another knitted socks, and those were all sent with him for his next life.

His body was flown into Fairbanks to be cremated, and I flew in, accompanied by Cheryl Folger, one of my very first students in the village, because my friends felt I shouldn't be left alone at that time. My friend Linda Swenson-Woods met me at the airport and took good care of me until Mom, Dad, and Sally arrived on the twenty-eighth. They came as soon as they could book a flight out of Kalamazoo. I know if it hadn't been for the love and support of my family and friends, I could not have gotten through that time.

My family and I stayed at Sophie's Station Hotel, and I was so happy and relieved to have my family around me. They just took over, especially Sally, and I didn't have to think about anything. I could just "be," which was all I could manage at the time.

The next day we had to spend in Fairbanks because that was the day Jerry was to be cremated. So again, with my family's help, I was able to tie up some loose ends, and then on Friday, we flew to Tanana. A group of Jerry's friends met us at the airport when we landed to carry his ashes to the Catholic church, where they remained until the service. The sisters had opened the church that afternoon specifically for that purpose.

The memorial service was held on October 1, 1993, and I was glad to have my family there for moral support, which I was in desperate need of at that time. Some of Jerry's friends came out from Fairbanks, Eagle River, Healy, and Nenana to pay their last respects, and the tribute was wonderful.

Out of respect for Jerry, the school closed on the day of the service, and because most of the town was in attendance, it was held at the community hall and was conducted by Sister Maria. A few of Jerry's closest friends, including Paul Starr and Pi, assisted with the Bible readings. I had chosen to include some of Jerry's favorite hymns and some of mine, and Earl Tumbloo carried the ashes into the room. All the veterans in town marched in, bearing the colors. Later I learned they did not fire the traditional twenty-one-gun salute as they thought that might upset me. I thanked them for their thoughtfulness.

Another of Jerry's good friends, David Solomon, wrote a special song in Jerry's honor, and he sang it at the service and accompanied it on his guitar. It was a very moving piece, and it meant a lot to David to be able to do that.

After the service, Sally and I, accompanied by a group of Jerry's buddies (Earl, David Sanders, Marty Scharff, and several others), took the container of ashes out into the woods in Tanana and scattered them. That was in keeping with Jerry's wishes, and it was then I knew that Jerry was finally at peace.

Mary and Paul Starr were a great support for me during that entire time. Cathy Fliris was very helpful to Mom and Dad during their stay in the village. Cynthia and Dale Erickson flew Mom, Dad, Sally, and I with Jerry's ashes from Fairbanks to Tanana and never charged a cent. Cynthia and the sisters prepared a wonderful collage of pictures for Jerry's memorial. I still don't know how they chose the pictures they did, but they had gone to our house while I was in Fairbanks and sorted through our many photos. It was a complete pictorial history of Jerry's life and a lovely gift for me. I could not have done a better job myself.

That evening, following the memorial service, the village held a funeral potlatch for Jerry. This was traditionally a native custom, and no one in the village could remember ever having a funeral potlatch to honor a white man before that time. But Jerry had been special. It seemed as if everybody in town had known and respected him. I never heard anyone say a bad word about my husband, and it was a very high native honor they were paying him by organizing this potlatch.

Jerry had done so many things for so many people; he hauled water for old ladies, he hauled wood for people who needed it, he was just always the person that was there to help out when anyone needed it. For several years, he had a rabbit snare line and donated the rabbits he caught to the Elder's Home in the village. All the residents were elderly natives, and they missed a lot of their native foods. So when Jerry brought rabbits and the cooks prepared them, making stew or soup, the elders were very grateful. Little things like that won Jerry the esteem of not only all the elders but also their families, which included most of the village residents.

The potlatch was steeped in many traditions, one of which was the serving of moose at the meal. Freddie Jordan and another man from the village had gone out and shot one for the occasion. Another custom was that the men would do all the cooking and preparation for the feast, and they outdid themselves, preparing not only roast moose but also the traditional moose soup. It would have been very discourteous and disrespectful not to try some of every dish offered to you, and there were too many to count. Also in keeping with tradition, I sat in the front row, surrounded by my family and Earl and Muriel, and we were served first.

The celebration was different than anything my family had ever seen before, and despite all the new and unfamiliar customs, they were very moved by the great love the people in Tanana had for Jerry and the tribute they paid him. It was a huge potlatch and one of the largest I ever attended in the village.

Following the potlatch, there was native dancing to accompany Jerry on his way to his new home. The dances were beautiful and authentic, handed down through many generations. Native drums accompanied each dance, and the dancers all wore native costumes. It was an eloquent, beautiful, and fitting tribute to Jerry, who in life had highly valued listening to and learning the native lore of Alaska.

CHAPTER 55

THE NEXT DAY, MOM AND Dad flew back to Fairbanks to the hotel. It was very difficult for them to get around in Tanana because it had snowed, and we thought they would be safer back in Fairbanks. My cousin Russ met them at the airport and took them to the hotel, and Earl and Muriel flew in with them and took care of them for me.

Sally and I stayed in Tanana for another day and packed up Jerry's clothes and possessions and did all the things that needed to be done following a death. Paul and Mary Starr and Cathy and Bill Fliris cleaned up our trailer for me, so I never had to deal with that. I will be eternally grateful to them for doing that. And again, Sally was there for me every step of the way, giving me moral support, which I definitely needed, and letting me cry when I needed to cry and laugh when I needed to laugh and just letting me be me.

The next day, she and I flew into Fairbanks, and that happened to be Sally's birthday, so we all went out to dinner at Pike's Landing. Then later that evening, we put Mom and Dad on a plane back to Michigan, but Sally stayed for the rest of the week, and I don't know what I ever would have done without her.

She checked my bank account, she called all my credit card companies and all sorts of places I couldn't have handled at that time, and sometimes she just let me talk. It was the worst of times; it was the best of times. And then on Friday of that week, Janie flew into Fairbanks and got off the plane, and Sally boarded the same plane and flew away. Janie stayed for the rest of the month of October. Again I thank God for the support of my family.

Jane helped me move into a new trailer in teacher housing, and what a job! But she organized it all. There she was telling them what to do, and she never once got angry with me. But I do remember her saying to me once, "Aunt Suie, don't you think you need a shower?"

And I did. I just hadn't thought of it. But mostly, Jane just did what I asked her to do. I probably asked her to do some pretty bizarre things, but she did them anyway, and I got moved in.

Teacher housing was nice because now I had running water and a flush toilet, and our trailer hadn't had those amenities. Jane helped me clean the new house and get organized and hang pictures and do all the little things that made a house a home.

While she was with me, we celebrated her birthday. I called Sally for the recipe of Jane's favorite gingerbread streusel cake, and I baked it for her. Then I arranged for a little surprise party. Mary Starr, Cathy Fliris, Deb Caudill, Sandy Mangold, and Ron Delay all attended, and Jane was so tickled to think that though she was five thousand miles from home, all these people had come with presents for her special day.

I can't even begin to tell you how helpful she was to me. I had taken several weeks off from school, but Jane wasn't about to let me sit around and get maudlin. Every day she had things for me to do. She would make a list of them, and by golly, together we got them done. She stayed through October 30, and on November 1, my nephew Kevin flew into Fairbanks. He was between jobs, so it worked out for both of us. I picked him up at the airport, and again, it seemed like God knew just what I needed and provided it.

CHAPTER 56

During Janie's visit, we put together a list of everything I'd need for my new place. That list included curtains and lamps, and since there was very little furniture in the place even though I had moved in some of my own, I needed some odds and ends. So Kevin and I went shopping to make my new place livable.

We also got weather-stripping and plastic film to winterize the windows. And Kevin, bless his heart, drove me all around Fairbanks like he had lived there forever. He picked up all the supplies and carted them around and got them to the airport for transport to Tanana. Even the furniture I wanted (a desk, a chest of drawers, bookcases, an entertainment center, and a couple of end tables), we got it all shipped. And then when we got back to Tanana, he had to put it all together. I really think both he and Janie had a fine time even though it was a working vacation for both of them.

Kevin stayed until the end of November and celebrated Thanksgiving Tanana-style, which was basically a traditional Thanksgiving but celebrated with other teachers who didn't have family in the village. It included the usual turkey with all the fixings but, for some reason, always included corn on the cob.

Kevin worked his fingers to the bone, helping me during the week, and then lay on the couch all day on Saturday and Sunday, watching football. He was just what I needed at that time. He was wonderful. He fixed all the things that needed to be fixed (the broken counter in the kitchen and leaky pipes), installed insulation in my porch, and even wallpapered for me, which he said he'd never done before. He hung more pictures up and sorted through Jerry's tools for me. I had no idea what many of the tools were, and he was very helpful in identifying them. He also helped me sort out Jerry's things, which had to be done, and was much easier to do with someone there. And he never complained no matter what I asked of him. All I had to do was cook him a good meal, like spaghetti or moose chops, and he was happy. And then, when I flew into Fairbanks with him and he left, I was totally alone for the first time in two months.

When I arrived back in Tanana, my friend Helena picked me up at the airstrip and dropped me off in front of my house. I remember getting out of the car and looking at my new home and thinking, *Okay, Lord. This is it. I can either go back in that house and crawl in my chair and sit there and feel sorry for myself, or I can go back in there and choose to live.*

My choice was to live. And it wasn't an easy time, but I can remember making the decision and consciously thanking Mom and Dad for raising me to believe in God. I know that he had a big part in helping me to make it through a very difficult time. I called on him often, and he was always there for me.

A couple weeks after Kevin left, I flew down to Las Vegas and spent Christmas with Mom, Dad, Sally, and Bud. That was a good time, and we had fun together doing different things and making new traditions.

When I got back to Tanana after Christmas, I was truly on my own, but I started right in, making a conscious effort to keep myself busy. I was involved with the Math Consortium and with writing a math curriculum for the state of Alaska. I was doing a lot of traveling, and almost every weekend, it seemed like I was in Fairbanks for one meeting or another.

Then in March, Jerry's sister, Sandy, came up for ten days. She seemed to need to have closure on his death, and I was glad to be able to talk with her and help her through it. The visit was good for both of us.

At the end of March, Kevin's eleven-year old son, Jamie, came up to spend some time with his great-aunt Suie. I'll tell you what—God does work in strange ways. I really needed Jamie and his wonderful sense of humor because, by that time, I was ready for some laughs. Believe me, he gave me plenty to laugh about with him. What a character. He could not only entertain himself, but he could entertain me too, and that was a tall order.

He played basketball on his knees with a tennis ball and two wastebaskets, and he'd go back and forth on his knees, playing both teams. It might have seemed silly, but it was fun to watch. While Jamie was in Tanana, we celebrated Easter. Since I didn't have kids to do baskets for, it was fun for me to fix one up. Even though he had already heard the truth about the Easter Bunny, he enjoyed finding a basket. I concocted a treasure hunt for him to find the goodies. He had to go all over, following my clues to locate his treasure. He also had received an Easter basket from his mom, so he had a fun time searching the house for his gifts, but he finally had them all and then proceeded to eat candy most of the day.

Well, he was just the pickup I needed. He was such a loving and sensitive child, and he brought a lot of joy to my life. It was a wonderful time, and everyone who met him loved him. My next-door neighbor Sandy thought he was great and wanted to adopt him.

One of the things that had tickled Jamie was that Sally (his Mimi) and I liked to leg wrestle. One evening, Sandy invited Jamie and me over for dinner, and after dinner, she asked him if there was anything he wanted to do. I knew he really just wanted to go home and go to bed because he was tired, but he said, "There is one thing. I want to see you and Aunt Suie leg wrestle." So we staged a leg-wrestling contest especially for him. I can't remember now who, if anyone, won, but I do know we laughed a lot.

Jamie stayed for almost two weeks, and I couldn't take any time off to accompany him back into Fairbanks, but Muriel Tumbloo picked him up at the airport and got him safely boarded on his plane home. When I tell you all my friends fell in love with my whole family, it's the truth, and Jamie was no exception.

About the middle of April, my longtime friend Laura Fuhrman-Hayes came to visit, and that was another thing that I needed. What a good friend she was. She came up for a week, and she didn't want to have anything to do with school, so she stayed home instead of accompanying me during the day. But she did all sorts of jobs for me while she was there. The kinds of things I'd been meaning to get to, like hanging the closet door, she did that. She sewed place mats for me to brighten up my table, and she even dusted. I loved it. Too bad she didn't come again. It was a joy having her there and talking about old times. We just enjoyed each other, and again, there was a lot of laughter. It was good for my soul.

After she left, there were only a few weeks of school left, and just before it dismissed for the summer, my brother and sister-in-law, Steve and Marti Nuyen, came up to visit. I was thrilled to see them because besides just wanting to see them, I was getting ready to have a garage sale and I had no idea about pricing for the boat and motor and the truck. Steve was a big help with that, and Marti was a born organizer. She pitched right in, and we sold everything I had for sale.

Marti was astounded because somebody actually bought two sheets of Styrofoam insulation. The teenager who bought it had been one of my old students whom I dearly loved, and Marti overheard him remark to his companion as he walked away, "Wow! I got a lifetime supply of toilet seats." She thought that was an odd thing until I explained that was what people used in their outhouses. You cut circles out to surround the holes so you didn't have to sit on the cold boards.

Steve and Marti had a good time while they were in Tanana. They stayed for about a week, and then we all flew into Fairbanks. I put them on the train to Denali, and I drove my little red truck down there to meet them at the train station. We stayed overnight at Rock Creek Bed and Breakfast, owned by Wayne and Lolita Valcq. The next day, we drove as far as we could into the park, about fifty or sixty miles, and they enjoyed that. We saw all sorts of animals, including an elusive albino moose.

Since the time of Jerry's death, my family ties have been strengthened. Each family member has been there to support me at just the time I needed it. I certainly can never repay them, and they have never asked to be repaid. But they all know that when the time comes and they need me, I will be there for each of them also.

CHAPTER 57

M Y DECISION TO REMAIN IN Tanana after Jerry died was a good one. Even though it was sometimes very difficult to have so many reminders, it helped me to work through my grief, and I made it.

The following spring, my friends Mary and Paul Starr bought a lovely riverboat and offered to transport their B & B guests upriver to visit some fish camps. Occasionally, Paul asked me to go along as a tour guide. What fun! The boat seated eight to ten people, and Paul took the groups about forty miles up the Yukon River to see how fish camps operated.

Cathy and Bill Fliris's camp was one of the stops, and there the Flirises showed the tourists how to cut and dry fish and how they canned the fish and how a fish wheel worked and how a smokehouse was run. And then we went on a little further up the river to what the locals called the Rapids. There, Stan and Kathleen Zuray had a fish camp, and Paul also stopped there for a short visit.

Each fish camp was totally unique in itself. Each seemed to have a personality of its own rather like different families. Sometimes we were lucky enough to see people actually fishing in the rapids. Mary always sent along a wonderful lunch for the group, and we ate on the boat as we floated with the motor off back down the Yukon River. How pleasant those sunny afternoons were; we chatted with the guests from all over the map. It seemed that almost every time Paul asked me to accompany him, the weather cooperated, and it was sunny and warm. I acted as tour guide several times a year for several years, and I really enjoyed it.

One time I went downriver with the Starrs to Georgina and Greg Wallace's fish camp, which was on an island in the Yukon near the village of Ruby. After visiting for a while with the Wallaces, we went on down the river to what was called the boneyard. The boneyard was a place where mastodons were alleged to have jumped over the cliff into the river, and there were mastodon bones embedded in the muskeg. Why the mastodons jumped off the high cliffs was anybody's guess, but as the river had eroded the bank, the bones had become more visible. It smelled pretty bad because once the bones emerged from the muskeg, they were not preserved any more, so they stunk. Sometimes you could see the bones sticking prominently out of the bank way up high, and some visitors tried to rope them to pull them out since they were valuable. What they failed to realize was, not only the bones but also the entire riverbank were owned by the Native Americans and the Antiquities Act of 1906 protects it. Tourists were not allowed to remove any of the embedded bones under penalty of law.

Once I remember going up the Yukon River and on up the Tanana River with Mary and Paul to a place called Hay Slough. We went way back in about ten or twenty miles to go blueberry picking. That was the best blueberry picking I've ever seen in my entire life and probably never will again. I sat in one place and never moved. I picked all the way around me, and I had a pail full of berries in an hour. And it was a big pail. That place was absolutely blue with berries. Paul, who was born and raised in the interior of Alaska, concurred. He'd never seen berries that thick either. And they were so juicy and sweet. Oh, we had a fun time that day.

I enjoyed a lot of fun trips with the Starrs. One time my friends Bette and John House-Myers, who had at one time taught in Tanana, were coming to visit. They were going to drive as far as Manley Hot Springs on the Tanana River, and Paul was to pick them up in the boat and take them to Bill and Cathy Fliris's fish camp. He invited me to go along, and I was excited since I had never been to Manley Hot Springs by boat before. What a lovely trip, and it was absolutely beautiful.

The Tanana River was very different from the Yukon River in that there were a lot of sand bars and was much shallower and quite murky with glacial runoff. All that silt turned the river's color to a muddy brown, but Paul was a very good navigator and actually was a boat pilot, so he knew what he was doing and our exact location at all times.

We picked up my friends, and I visited with them all the way back downriver to the Flirises' camp, which took about three hours, so we had a lot of time to catch up on one another's lives. At the confluence of the Yukon and Tanana Rivers, the weather turned nasty, and the waves were huge. It was like being on the ocean in very bad weather, which I had experienced before. It got pretty scary, and there was dead silence in the boat while we rode out the storm. We were really being slapped around, and Paul wasn't even sure he could make it to Cathy and Bill's, but with his expertise, we finally did. Paul and I were invited in for supper and had some tea and then got back in the boat for the return trip to Tanana.

I was not looking forward to it after our earlier experience, but by the time we got back to the confluence, where the waves had plagued us before, the water was flat, calm, and glassy, like a mirror. The weather can change the personality of the rivers very quickly and you learn to respect that really fast.

PART VII

THE HEALY STORY
AND
THE END OF THE STORY

B ACK IN THE FALL OF 1986, Jerry had gone caribou hunting with Pi, and as they were driving down the Parks Highway near Healy, Jerry noticed a piece of property for sale on the Nenana River. So they stopped to check it out, and he fell in love with the location, so we bought it with the understanding we would retire there when I was done teaching. The lot had come from a bigger homestead property owned by Mike Combs, and he wanted to split it up and sell it off.

The property was located at Rock Creek, which was thirteen miles north of Healy, Alaska, and finally, I would have a home "on the highway system." It was a beautiful, peaceful spot, and I loved it. In 1987 we put in a foundation for our home. Jerry had a temporary walled tent built on the lot for us to stay in while we were working on our house. The tent was like a little cabin and had a bed, a dresser, and a table. There was even a small counter space in the kitchen and a wood-burning stove for heat. Back further on the property, he dug an outhouse. What more could we want? It was quite a comfortable home for the summer months. It had a porch on the front, and Jerry built a picnic table and bought a hammock for lazy summer afternoons.

Building the outhouse was a learning experience since when he started to dig the hole for it, he found he was in the permafrost layer. The hole just kept falling in on itself, so he ended up relocating it altogether.

The second summer, Jerry put up another smaller walled tent for storage, complete with its own wood-burning stove. We also cleared a driveway into the property, and that involved a lot of brush cutting.

We had some really good times in Healy. Our good friends Pi and Linda lived there, and they sometimes let us take showers at their place because we didn't have running water in our tent. We did have a well dug that year though by a man from Canada who traveled around, putting in wells for a living. He did a good job, and we were glad to have running water. Well, we had running water if we pumped it. That was a great improvement.

We had some wonderful neighbors: Wayne and Lolita Valcq (who ran the Rock Creek Bed & Breakfast), Jim and Nan Blakeway (with their brood of four young children), Mike and Barb Combs. It was a pleasant little community, and we really looked forward to our summers there.

Since our lot was in the woods, we shared our space with a lot of wildlife. We often watched the antics of a mama moose and her calf as well as several different kinds of bears. Jerry bought a big bear gun and insisted I learned how to shoot because sometimes I stayed at the tent by myself. So he took me to a big open gravel pit and proceeded to teach me how to use the weapon.

Now I had used guns before, and I'm a pretty good shot, but I didn't realize how powerful this gun was. I took aim and pulled the trigger. The recoil knocked me to the ground, and the gun went flying out of my hands. Jerry really got mad and accused me of deliberately throwing the gun down. All I could do was sit there and cry. I said, "Geez! I didn't throw the gun down. The gun threw me down." Needless to say, I never got another gun lesson, and fortunately, I never had an opportunity to need that knowledge.

Sometimes we just got in the truck and went riding around the Healy area, and that was always fun to do because there were so many roads to explore. The Usibelli Coal Mine was just outside Healy, and the mine had constructed many of the roads to bring in supplies and machinery, so we explored most of those. We always saw lots of wildflowers and wildlife on the back roads, so there was always something to investigate. Sometimes I packed a picnic lunch, and we went berry picking up in the Healy River valley. It seemed like every time we went out, we sighted at least one moose.

We often visited Ferry, a little town just across the Nenana River from Healy. The only way to get to Ferry was across the railroad bridge, so we parked on one side of the river and walked across the trestle. There were a lot of old abandoned mines in that area, and I think we inspected them all.

Sometimes we just drove down the Parks Highway to the canyon just outside the entrance of Denali National Park. The locals call that spot Glitter Gulch because that is where all the tourists hang out. It is even more developed now with souvenir shops and restaurants, so there's even more glitz and activity in that area.

Healy was the first place we ever had a real mailbox other than a post office box, and that was pretty exciting for me because it meant we actually belonged someplace. Our mailbox was located out on the highway about a mile and a half from our home, so Jerry bought me a bike, and every day, I got to make the trip to pick up the mail. That was a nice ride, but sometimes I met a moose on the trail, so I turned around and made Jerry go get the mail!

One of the coolest things about living in that particular spot was all the wildflowers growing there. I love wildflowers, and they thrived all over our property—fireweed, columbine, and lupine just to name a few. So Jerry bought me a flower book so I could learn to identify them all and learn their names. I made notations in the book under the flower about where I had seen it and the date. My goal was to see and identify every one of the flowers in that book. I haven't quite reached my goal yet, but I had seen a lot of them in the years I've called Alaska home.

In the summer of 1988, Bud came up for two weeks to help us work on the house at Healy. He helped Jerry get the roof on and helped with a lot of other things that I couldn't help with. That was really fun, having him around. Bud and I had cribbage tournaments, and he won most of them because I wasn't much of a challenge since I didn't play too well. We also took him fishing in our spare time, and he and Jerry went white-water rafting in Nenana. I remember watching them from the bridge, and it looked like they were having great fun.

Our house was really cute although it was quite small. There was a living room, a dining area, a kitchen, and a real bathroom on the first floor. A circular stairway led upstairs to a dormered loft, and that would be the bedroom. We never finished the house, and in the summer of 1993, we sold it to our neighbors Tom and Jureen Howarth, who still live there and let me visit occasionally. I like that, but sometimes it's hard because there are so many memories of Jerry. But it was a fun time and a fun chapter in our lives, and I enjoyed it very much.

In the summer of 1989, Mom and Dad and Sal and Bud and Ward and Barb Healy (no relationship to the town of Healy) came up to visit us. Mom and Dad stayed in their motorhome, and the others had reserved a cabin at Rock Creek Bed and Breakfast. Jerry carved out a path from our house over to Wayne and Lolita's. He even built a little footbridge so when they crossed Rock Creek to our house, they wouldn't get their little tootsies wet.

We had good times doing all the tourist things and even did some things that ordinary tourists would not have the opportunity to do. Sally, Barb, Mom, Dad, and I flew into Tanana so they could see how we lived most of the year. I introduced them to lots of people in the village and made a feast for them of moose, ptarmigan, bear, and other animals that weren't served commonly in the Lower 48.

We all picnicked at June Creek near Healy on the Fourth of July and waded in the icy waters to cool off from the ninety-degree temperatures we were having at that time.

We took a scenic tour on the Riverboat Discovery down the Nenana River, and Barb and Ward and Sally and Bud and I took the white-water raft ride on the Nenana River. Mom, Dad, and Jerry waved to us from the highway bridge as we were being swept and tossed by the bucking river. The captain told us that some of the rafts, which were made of rubber, were self-bailing and then announced the bad news, "This one is not."

So we all had buckets, and we bailed water in between times of clinging to the sides of the raft for dear life. Oh, it was a trip! That was my first experience, and I hate to confess this, but it was also my last.

We had a lot of fun sightseeing that summer, and the time seemed to go too quickly as it always did when you were enjoying yourself.

CHAPTER 59

I N JANUARY OF 1999, I decided twenty-six years of teaching was enough and it was time for me to retire. So in March, I wrote my letter to the Tanana School Board, telling them of my intentions, and as fate would have it, my fifty-second birthday, May 6, 1999, was my last day of teaching.

I have to admit that I'm glad I retired and I would never go back; it was the end of an era. I spent seventeen years in Tanana, and I absolutely loved what I did. I know I made the right decision when I chose to become a teacher, but I also know that I made the right decision when I retired. It was time.

I began in January to make plans for my retirement. My plan was, I would move into Fairbanks and get an apartment and take some time deciding what I wanted to do from there. So I flew to town at the end of March and found a two-bedroom apartment on the third floor at Sophie's Plaza, and I rented it. When I got back to Tanana, I began to wonder about the practicality of having a place on the third floor. I called back to the manager of the apartment and was told there was a first-floor apartment available, and since I hadn't yet moved in, there would be no extra charge.

It was a wonderful place, and I had some wonderful neighbors. I was able to rent it on April 1. So twice during April, I flew into Fairbanks, and each time, I took some of my belongings with me. I got the telephone hooked up and the mail situated, and then I went back to Tanana and packed up more of my things. Then I sent them, by mail, into town, and my friend Muriel Tumbloo picked them up from the post office and carted them over to my new home.

I packed my entire fifty-two years of life into forty-two boxes, and I remember calling my sister to reflect on that fact and to decide whether I should laugh or cry over it. I was able to sell a lot of my things, and the school district bought my furniture. My friends Dale and Cynthia Erickson flew my last load of stuff—my television, my sewing machine, and my rocking chair, which Jerry had bought, into Fairbanks for me. They stored it at their hangar until I could pick it up.

I arrived in my retirement home on May 8, 1999, at two o'clock in the afternoon, and at eight o'clock that same night, my mom flew in. She stayed with me for three weeks and helped me unpack and get settled. We had a great time.

The following Sunday was Mother's Day, and I knew Mom would want to go to church, so we found our way to the First Methodist Church of Fairbanks. I had been searching for a church home, I found it right then and there, and I've been there ever since.

I found I absolutely loved living in Fairbanks. It was not too big, and I knew enough about the town that I felt comfortable, so I was really happy. I had some friends there, and I met a lot of new friends. I had a wonderful next-door neighbor, Mary Gilbert, who turned out to be a very good friend and a wellspring of information about Fairbanks. I made friends at the church and began creating a little niche for myself.

That first year, I was asked to come out of retirement to work with student teachers that were placed in different schools to do their internships. I was to be their mentor and critique them two times during a semester. I enjoyed starting new teachers on their way to what I hoped would be as productive and satisfying a career as I'd had.

At the church, I also met Lois Patton, who had joined the congregation about the same time I had, and that common bond made us friends. She suggested we attend the 40 Plus Singles' Club the church sponsored. She'd heard they held dances, and she loved to dance. I, on the other hand, was not ready for anything like that, and I told her so. Now, Lois was very persistent. She started mentioning this idea in September, and finally, in March, she had succeeded in breaking down all my excuses. I reluctantly agreed to go with her one time.

The first meeting was not a dance but a breakfast gathering at a Fairbanks restaurant called the Cookie Jar. When I looked around at the group, I thought, *What am I doing here with all these old people?* But Lois wasn't finished. She kept after me until I agreed to go with her to a St. Patrick's Day dinner dance at the Eagle's Hall, hosted by the 40 Plus Club.

It turned out that Lois's main interest was finding a man for herself. I, on the other hand, was perfectly happy with my life just the way it was playing out. Wouldn't you know it? That was the night I met John Curtis. We hit it off right away. We started dancing, and the next day, he called and asked me out. And the rest, as they say, is history. John and I dated for about a year and two months, and then we got married.

Perhaps my greatest regret in my life was the fact that I never had any children, but I surrounded myself with them during my entire teaching career. On the day I married John, I not only got a new husband but I also got four children as well, and they are wonderful.

Eventually we bought our own home here in Fairbanks, and I love living here. I love being retired. My life as a teacher was something that I thoroughly enjoyed, but retirement is just as much fun. And looking back, I don't know how I ever had time to work.

Bathtub water in Kaltag. 1980

Bigfoot Footprints
Savoonga
Practical Joke

Christmas
Savoonga 1978
Note size of tree

Showdrift at House
(Christmas Time)
Suzanne Dec 1977

Presbyterian Church
Savoonga 1978

Kaltag Students Dancing at Festival of Native Arts
Suzanne made Kuspuks
1982
Fairbanks

House Savoonga
Aug 1977

High and dry on uncharted rock near Juneau
May 1982

Jerry & Mitch on day Suie got teaching job in Kaltag
June 1980
Near Healy, AK

Ramon's Flying Service
Suzanne & Mitch just before leaving Savoonga
May 1979

Mitch
Summer 1978

"Observer" at Anchor, British Columbia 1981
U.S.C.G DOC. # 637634
Gerald & Suzanne Henning
Kaltag, Alaska 99748
Nanimo, BC

Tent home at Rock Creek
Summer 1986

Savoonga Ladies picking opahs (sea foods)
Fall 1977

Savoonga & Ice pack from mountains

Sitka off bridge
1973

Our boat & the Dentist boat tied up at Tenakee Springs
Summer 1982

Suzanne the day she got her teaching job in Kaltag.
June 1980
Near Healy, AK

Inside of Tent Home
Rock Creek 1986

Thanksgiving dinner!
Sitka 1973

Top Fish 28 lbs
2nd Fish 25 lbs
Halibut 10 lbs
Sitka 1975

Walrus gut and walrus ribs
used for toys for kids
Savoonga 1977

Opahs! Upclose
Savoonga 1977

Gordon Alceya
Big Big Walrus Head
Savoonga 1977

After!
Winter 1977

ABOUT THE AUTHOR

Sally Mahieu was born and raised in Southwest Michigan. She is the eldest of three children, one of whom is the subject of this book. After attending Western Michigan University, she received a writing degree from Famous Writers School in Westport, Connecticut. She has written for local, regional, and national publications. Sally is a former freelance writer for the *Kalamazoo Gazette*.

She is married to her husband, Edward. Sally has two adult children, two adult grandsons, and two beautiful great-granddaughters.

She's still deeply rooted in Kalamazoo, Michigan, and lives in the house that her great-great-grandfather built in 1896.

Lightning Source UK Ltd.
Milton Keynes UK
UKHW041258240819
348502UK00002B/660/P